lonely planet

D1259806

Pocket

HELSINKI

TOP SIGHTS • LOCAL LIFE • MADE EASY

Mara Vorhees, Catherine Le Nevez

In This Book

QuickStart Guide

Your keys to understanding the city – we help you decide what to do and how to do it

Need to Know
Tips for a smooth trip

Neighbourhoods
What's where

Explore Helsinki

The best things to see and do, neighbourhood by neighbourhood

Top Sights
Make the most of your visit

Local Life
The insider's city

The Best of Helsinki

The city's highlights in handy lists to help you plan

Best Walks
See the city on foot

Helsinki's Best...
The best experiences

Survival Guide

Tips and tricks for a seamless, hassle-free city experience

Getting Around
Travel like a local

Essential Information
Including where to stay

Our selection of the city's best places to eat, drink and experience:

◉ **Sights**

✖ **Eating**

🚱 **Drinking**

⭐ **Entertainment**

🔓 **Shopping**

These symbols give you the vital information for each listing:

☏ Telephone Numbers	👶 Family-Friendly
⊙ Opening Hours	🐾 Pet-Friendly
P Parking	🚍 Bus
🚭 Nonsmoking	🛳 Ferry
@ Internet Access	Ⓜ Metro
☎ Wi-Fi Access	Ⓢ Subway
🥗 Vegetarian Selection	🚋 Tram
🖹 English-Language Menu	🚆 Train

Find each listing quickly on maps for each neighbourhood:

Bar Hemingway

16 🚇 Map p233, B2

Legend has it that Hemi
self, wielding a machine
erate this timber-pan
ered bar during
showpiece is a
en by Papa ar
s.com; Hôtel Rit
⊙6.30pm-2a

Lonely Planet's Helsinki

Lonely Planet Pocket Guides are designed to get you straight to the heart of the city.

Inside you'll find all the must-see sights, plus tips to make your visit to each one really memorable. We've split the city into easy-to-navigate neighbourhoods and provided clear maps so you'll find your way around with ease. Our expert authors have searched out the best of the city: walks, food, nightlife and shopping, to name a few. Because you want to explore, our 'Local Life' pages will take you to some of the most exciting areas to experience the real Helsinki.

And of course you'll find all the practical tips you need for a smooth trip: itineraries for short visits, how to get around, and how much to tip the guy who serves you a drink at the end of a long day's exploration.

It's your guarantee of a really great experience.

Our Promise

You can trust our travel information because Lonely Planet authors visit the places we write about, each and every edition. We never accept freebies for positive coverage, so you can rely on us to tell it like it is.

QuickStart Guide 6

Helsinki Top Sights 8
Helsinki Local Life 12
Helsinki Day Planner 14
Need to Know 16
Helsinki Neighbourhoods 18

Explore Helsinki 20

22 City Centre

38 Kruununhaka & Katajanokka

54 Punavuori & Ullanlinna

76 Kamppi & Töölö

102 Kallio

Worth a Trip:

Suomenlinna 50
Seurasaaren Ulkomuseo 100
Porvoo 112
Tuusulanjärvi 114

The Best of Helsinki 116

Helsinki's Best Walks

Architectural Stroll..............................118

Green Helsinki....................................120

Helsinki's Best ...

Eating...122

Drinking & Nightlife...........................124

Entertainment....................................126

Shopping..128

History...130

Art & Architecture.............................132

Outdoors..134

Saunas...135

For Kids..136

For Free...137

Tours..138

Survival Guide 139

Before You Go.....................139

Arriving in Helsinki.............141

Getting Around...................142

Essential Information.........143

Language............................146

Sky Wheel (p46)
ABB PHOTO/SHUTTERSTOCK ©

QuickStart Guide

Helsinki Top Sights 8

Helsinki Local Life 12

Helsinki Day Planner 14

Need to Know 16

Helsinki Neighbourhoods 18

Welcome to Helsinki

Spectacularly entwined with the Baltic's bays, inlets and islands, Helsinki's boulevards and backstreets are awash with magnificent architecture, enticing eateries and groundbreaking design. This modern city by the sea is less flashy than the other Nordic capitals, but rivals them for accessibility, creativity and quirkiness.

Sibelius Monument (p90) © Eila Hiltunen/KUVASTO.
KIEV.VICTOR/SHUTTERSTOCK © LICENSED BY VISCOPY, 2017

Helsinki
Top Sights

Suomenlinna (p50)

Finland's mighty island-set fortress.

Design Museum (p56)

A showcase for Finnish design.

Seurasaaren Ulkomuseo (p100)

Historic outdoor museum filled with wooden buildings.

Ateneum (p24)

Finland's premier art gallery.

Kajsaniemi (p28)

Helsinki's harbourside botanic gardens.

Kiasma (p26)

Avant-garde art and cultural hub.

Tennispalatsi (p80)

Cultural centre and art museum.

Kansallismuseo (p78)

Finland's blockbuster historical museum.

Helsinki
Local Life

Local experiences and hidden gems
to help you uncover the real city

It won't take long to discover what Stadilainen (Helsinki residents) love about their hometown when you explore its rich maritime heritage, its super-cool design district, its offbeat outskirts and its happening nightlife.

Maritime Helsinki (p40)

☑ Icebreakers
☑ Harbourfront warehouses

Design District (p58)

☑ Design shopping
☑ Designer dining

Marimekko store

Helsinki by Night (p82)

☑ Glow-in-the-dark minigolf ☑ Live music

Other great places to experience the city like a local:

Jääpuisto (p33)

La Torrefazione (p34)

Kauppatori (p48)

Löyly Sauna (p65)

Konepahalli (p70)

Hietaranta (p89)

Kotiharjun Sauna (p108)

Kallio Block Party (p111)

Creative Kallio (p104)

☑ Public art ☑ Industrial spaces

Helsinki
Day Planner

Day One

If you're arriving by rail, Helsinki's central **train station** (p141) gives you an immediate feel for the city's stunning National Romantic art nouveau architecture. From here it's just footsteps to **Kiasma** (p26) to catch modern and contemporary Finnish and international art in striking contemporary surrounds. More art is on display at the nearby **Ateneum** (p24), Helsinki's – and Finland's – premier showcase for the country's 'golden age' from the late 19th century through to the 1950s.

Lunch at the **Karl Fazer Café** (p33) is a Helsinki institution. Afterwards, stroll through the city's central strip of green, **Esplanadin Puisto** (p31), and visit central Finnish design shops. Continue your stroll through the city's beautiful botanic gardens, **Kajsaniemi** (p28), and its 10 interlinked greenhouses.

Book ahead to take in a concert at the **Musiikkitalo** (p35), which hosts everything from classical to jazz, rock and pop. Even if you don't catch a performance, its bar is a great place for a nightcap.

Day Two

Get an early start to beat the crowds at Helsinki's Lutheran cathedral, **Tuomiokirkko** (p45), a masterpiece from architect CL Engel, then head to another resplendent church, the Finnish Orthodox **Uspenskin Katedraali** (p45), built as a Russian Orthodox cathedral and still topped by its distinctive gold onion domes.

Make reservations ahead for Michelin-starred modern Finnish cuisine at **Olo** (p46). After lunch, make your way to Helsinki's main market square, the **kauppatori** (p48), and board a local ferry bound for **Suomenlinna** (p141), the 'fortress of Finland', set over a series of islands in Helsinki's archipelago. Spend the afternoon exploring its fortifications, bunkers and numerous museums. Highlights here include scrambling through the Vesikko, the only WWII-era submarine remaining in Finland.

For dinner, feast on game platters and house-brewed beers at **Suomenlinnan Panimo** (p125). Return by ferry to the kauppatori. Take in a stunning panorama of Helsinki aboard the **Sky Wheel** (p46) then finish with a swim and/or a sauna at waterfront swimming complex **Allas Sea Pool** (p41), which also has dazzling skyline views.

Short on time?

We've arranged Helsinki's must-sees into these day-by-day itineraries to make sure you see the very best of the city in the time you have available.

Day Three

☀ Take a ferry from the kauppatori to the island of Seurasaari. Its delightful open-air museum, **Seurasaaren Ulkomuseo** (p101), shelters a collection of 87 historic wooden buildings relocated to the island from around Finland. Bring provisions for a picnic lunch on the island, or head to a cafe here.

☀ Return by bus and make your way to the rock-hewn church **Temppeliaukion Kirkko** (p89) with its stunning copper roof and sublime acoustics (check the agenda to try to align your visit with a concert). Afterwards wander through the **Kansallismuseo** (p78) to learn about Finnish history or check out contemporary-art exhibitions inside the **Tennispalatsi** (p80) at the **Helsinki Art Museum** (p81).

☾ Enjoy a post-dinner glass of wine at **Vin-Vin** (p94) or a sensational cocktail at steampunk-themed **Steam Hellsinki** (p94), before catching a film at the art deco **Orion Theatre** (p96) or jazz at Helsinki's best jazz club, **Storyville** (p98).

Day Four

☀ Kick-start your day with a coffee and pastry at Helsinki's historic market hall, **Vanha Kauppahalli** (p65), before making your way to the city's **Design Museum** (p56). Glassware by Aino Aalto, a Paimio bent birch plywood chair by Alvar Aalto and a semi-spherical fibreglass Ball chair by Eero Aarniio are among its iconic designs. Be sure to get a combination ticket for the neighbouring **Museum of Finnish Architecture** (p62).

☀ Lunch is designer Finnish dishes at **Juuri** (p68). Then flex your credit card at the **Design District shops** (p58). While away the afternoon in the seaside park **Kaivopuisto** (p64) and relax afterwards with a sauna at **Löyly Sauna** (p65).

☾ For dinner, check out more of Alvar and Aino Aalto's work while dining at the **Savoy** (p66). Then make your way to the creative neighbourhood of **Kallio** (p102) to check out its nightlife – the streets of Helsinginkatu and Vaasankatu in particular have plenty of buzzing bars. End the night at top Helsinki club **Kuudes Linja** (p110), famed for experimental beats.

Need to Know

For more information, see Survival Guide (p139)

Currency
Euro (€)

Language
Finnish, Swedish (official); English widely spoken

Visas
Generally not required for stays of up to 90 days; some nationalities will need a Schengen visa.

Money
Credit cards are widely accepted. ATMs (bearing the name 'Otto') are prevalent. There are currency-exchange counters at all transport terminals; visit www.forex.fi to locate others.

Mobile Phones
Purchasing a Finnish SIM card at any R-kioski shop for your own phone (provided it's unlocked) is cheapest. Top the credit up at the same outlets, online or at ATMs. Roaming charges within the EU have been abolished.

Time
Eastern European Time (EET; UTC/GMT plus two hours)

Tipping
Service is considered to be included in bills, so there's no need to tip at all unless you want to reward exceptional service.

❶ Before You Go

Your Daily Budget

Budget: Less than €120
► Dorm bed: €25–35
► City Bike per 30 minutes: free
► Lunch buffet: €8–14

Midrange: €120–250
► Standard hotel double room: €100–160
► Two-course meal with wine: €50–80
► Public transport day ticket: €9

Top End: More than €250
► Suite in boutique hotel: from €185
► Degustation menu with wine: from €80
► Taxi ride across town: €25–40

Useful Websites

Visit Helsinki (www.visithelsinki.fi) Excellent tourist-board website.

City of Helsinki (www.hel.fi) Helsinki City website, with many useful links.

Lonely Planet (www.lonelyplanet.com/finland) Destination information, hotel bookings, traveller forum and more.

HSL/HRT (www.hsl.fi) Public-transport information and journey planner.

Advance Planning

Three months before Book your hotel, especially if you'll be visiting at peak times or during festivals.

Two months before Check entertainment calendars and buy tickets.

Two weeks before Make dinner reservations at your must-eat restaurants.

One week before Reserve boat cruises and/or guided walking or cycling tours.

2 Arriving in Helsinki

✈ Helsinki-Vantaa Airport

The airport–city rail link (www.hsl.f; €5, 30 minutes, 5.05am to 12.05am) serves Helsinki's train station. The airport is also linked to central Helsinki by bus, including fast Finnair buses (€6.30, 30 minutes, every 20 minutes, 5am to midnight), and taxis; a Taksi Helsinki cab costs around €45 to €50.

🚌 Kamppi Bus Station

International and long-distance domestic buses arrive at Kamppi bus station in Kamppi, at the city centre's southwestern edge, which has its own metro station (Kamppi stop).

🚌 Helsinki Train Station

Helsinki's central train station, serving international and domestic trains, is linked to the metro (Rautatientori stop).

⚓ Ferry Terminals

Helsinki's five international ferry terminals are all served by tram (or bus and metro).

3 Getting Around

🚲 Bicycle

Helsinki's shared-bike scheme, City Bikes (www.hsl.fi/citybikes), has some 1500 bikes at 150 stations citywide.

⚓ Boat

Local ferries serve Suomenlinna and Helsinki Zoo, among other island destinations.

🚌 Bus

Most visitors won't need to use buses, which serve the northern suburbs, Espoo and Vantaa.

Ⓜ Metro

Helsinki's single, forked metro line has 17 stations. Most are beyond the centre; the most useful for visitors are in the centre and Kallio.

🚕 Taxi

Hail cabs on the street or at taxi stands, or phone Taksi Helsinki (☎010-00700; www.taksihelsinki.fi).

🚋 Tram

Ten main routes cover the city. Three of these, trams 2, 4 and 6, can double as budget sightseeing tours.

Helsinki
Neighbourhoods

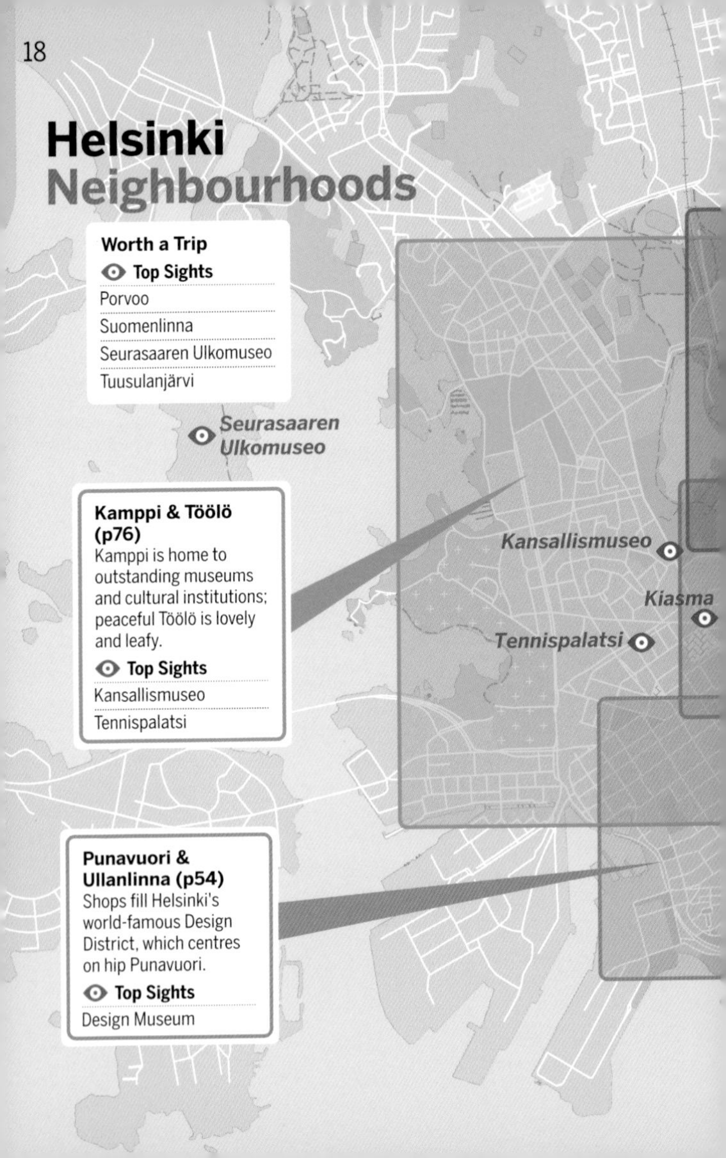

Worth a Trip
⊙ **Top Sights**

Porvoo

Suomenlinna

Seurasaaren Ulkomuseo

Tuusulanjärvi

⊙ *Seurasaaren Ulkomuseo*

Kamppi & Töölö (p76)
Kamppi is home to outstanding museums and cultural institutions; peaceful Töölö is lovely and leafy.

⊙ **Top Sights**

Kansallismuseo

Tennispalatsi

Kansallismuseo ⊙

Kiasma ⊙

Tennispalatsi ⊙

Punavuori & Ullanlinna (p54)
Shops fill Helsinki's world-famous Design District, which centres on hip Punavuori.

⊙ **Top Sights**

Design Museum

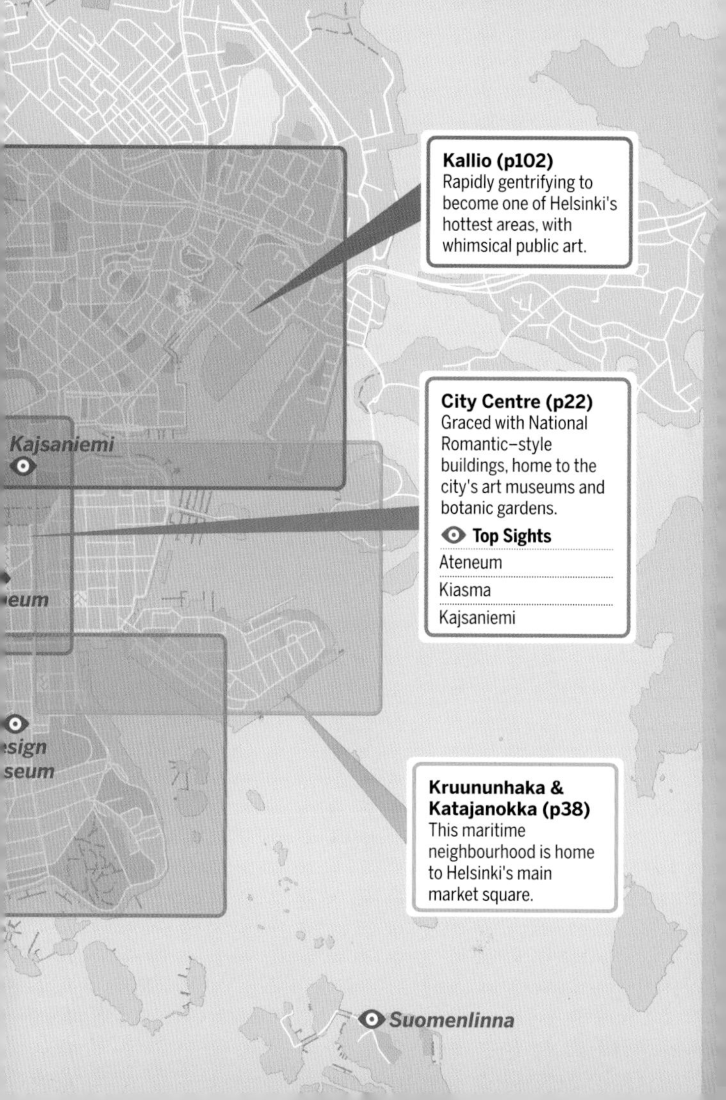

Kallio (p102)
Rapidly gentrifying to become one of Helsinki's hottest areas, with whimsical public art.

City Centre (p22)
Graced with National Romantic–style buildings, home to the city's art museums and botanic gardens.

◎ Top Sights

Ateneum

Kiasma

Kajsaniemi

Kruununhaka & Katajanokka (p38)
This maritime neighbourhood is home to Helsinki's main market square.

Kajsaniemi
⊙

eum

⊙
sign
seum

⊙ *Suomenlinna*

Explore
Helsinki

City Centre 22

Kruununhaka & Katajanokka 38

Punavuori & Ullanlinna 54

Kamppi & Töölö 76

Kallio 102

Worth a Trip

Suomenlinna 50
Seurasaaren
Ulkomuseo 100
Porvoo 112
Tuusulanjärvi 114

Colourful waterfront buildings in Kruununhaka (p38)
SCANRAIL/GETTY IMAGES ©

Explore

City Centre

Helsinki's elegant city centre is graced with beautiful buildings in National Romantic style, Finland's distinctive interpretation of art nouveau. While it's primarily a place of business and commerce, there are some standout attractions for visitors, including major museums and beautiful botanic gardens.

The Sights in a Day

☀️ Spend the morning browsing the challenging contemporary exhibits at **Kiasma** (p26), or the glorious 'golden age' of Finnish art at the **Ateneum** (p24). Afterwards, stroll down **Esplanadin Puisto** (pictured, left; p31) and do a spot of shopping at innovative shops like **Artek** (p36) and **Tre** (p36).

☀️ Stop along the way for lunch at the classic **Karl Fazer Café** (p33). Then your afternoon is free to wander the 4-hectare **Kajsaniemi** (p28), its gardens and greenhouses bursting with plantlife.

☾ In the evening, you might catch a concert at the majestic **Musiikkitalo** (p35). Or for a less formal evening, snag a spot on the terrace at **Kappeli** (p34) and watch the folks strolling on the Esplanadi.

🔘 Top Sights

Ateneum (p24)

Kiasma (p26)

Kajsaniemi (p28)

💜 Best of the City Centre

Eating
Karl Fazer Café (p33)

Drinking
Kappeli (p34)

La Torrefazione (p34)

Shopping
Artek (p36)

Stockmann (p37)

Getting There

Ⓜ **Metro** Metro station Rautatientori is linked to Helsinki's central train station (p31). Services on Helsinki's single-line metro head west (via Kamppi) and northeast (via Kallio) to the outer suburbs.

🚋 **Tram** Trams 4 and 5 serve Katajanokka. Lines 1, 2, 3, 6 and 10 serve Punavuori and Ullanlinna. Line 7 serves Kruununhaka and Kallio. Lines 3, 6 and 9 also serve Kallio. Lines 7 and 9 serve Kamppi, while lines 1, 2, 4 and 10 serve Töölö. All lines pass close to the train station.

Top Sights
Ateneum

Over 4300 paintings and 750 sculptures spanning the mid-18th century to the 1950s are contained within the collection of the Ateneum, Finland's premier art gallery. Set in a monumental 1887-completed building, this is the number-one stop to learn about Finnish art, with context provided by some 650 prized works by international artists, including the first-ever museum-acquired Van Gogh.

The Building
The palatial three-storey building housing the Ateneum was designed by Finnish architect

◉ Map p30, C4

www.ateneum.fi

Kaivokatu 2

adult/child €15/free

🕑 10am-6pm Tue & Fri, to 8pm Wed & Thu, to 5pm Sat & Sun

'Stories of Finnish Art' exhibition

Theodor Höijer in neo-Renaissance style, and built between 1885 and 1887. The Finnish Art Society held its first exhibition here in 1888.

The building is named for the Greek goddess of the arts, Athena. Above the main entrance, look for busts of Italian Renaissance architect Donato Bramante and painter and architect Raphael, and Greek sculptor, painter and architect Phidias.

Finnish Collections

Finnish paintings and sculptures from the 'golden age' of the late 19th century through to the 1950s include works by the nation's most important artists.

The undisputed highlight is the prolific Akseli Gallen-Kallela's triptych from Finland's national epic, the *Kalevala*. Titled *The Aino Myth* (1891) it depicts Väinämöinen's pursuit of the maiden Aino.

Eagle at a Cliff's Edge (1880) by Ferdinand von Wright, *The Wounded Angel* (1903) by Hugo Simberg, *Women Outside the Church at Ruokolahti* (1887) by Albert Edelfelt, *Under the Yoke* (1893) by Eero Järnefelt, *The Convalescent* (1888) by Helene Schjerfbeck and *Pioneers in Karelia* (1900) by Pekka Halonen are other must-sees.

International Collections

The Ateneum's collection of 19th- and early-20th-century foreign art includes *Street in Auvers-sur-Oise* (1890) by Vincent van Gogh. Purchased in 1903, it was the world's first-ever Van Gogh painting to be acquired by a museum, which exemplifies the visionary nature of the gallery that endures today.

Also here are *The Road Bridge at L'Estaque* (1879) by Paul Cézanne, *Portrait of the Artist Léopold Survage* (1918) by Amedeo Modigliani and *Landscape with a Pig and a Horse* (1903) by Paul Gauguin, among other standouts.

☑ **Top Tips**

▶ Workshops (free with admission) for all ages take place every Saturday in English from 11am to 2pm, and might be on watercolour painting, jewellery making, drawing or textile printing – check the agenda online.

▶ One-hour guided tours in English (included in admission) take place at noon on the second and fourth Sunday of the month.

▶ There's a good bookshop and reading room on the ground floor.

✕ Take a Break

On the ground floor, the elegant Ateneum Bistro cafe-restaurant, serving contemporary twists on Finnish classics, closes one hour before the museum does.

Finnish pastries are tantalisingly displayed at nearby bakery Kanniston Leipomo (p34), which has on-site seating.

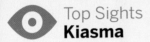

Top Sights
Kiasma

Unveiled just before the turn of the millennium, Kiasma is a beacon of Helsinki's progressiveness, from its dazzling metallic building to the ground-breaking contemporary-art exhibitions, including cutting-edge digital art, and public spaces that have made it a focal point of the city's cultural and social life, with a packed program of special events and fantastic amenities for kids.

The Building
In 1992 US architect Steven Holl's winning design was chosen from 516 entries in a competition to

◉ Map p30, A3

www.kiasma.fi

Mannerheiminaukio 2

adult/child €14/free, 1st Sun of month free

⊙10am-5pm Tue & Sun, to 8.30pm Wed-Fri, to 6pm Sat

create a contemporary-art museum in Helsinki. Holl was fascinated by Finland's natural light and utilised curved zinc, aluminium, brass and glass to capture it in the building's curvaceous facade and its white plaster interior walls contrasted by dark concrete floors. Work began in 1996 and it opened to the public in 1998.

The museum ranges over five floors, with a contemporary theatre hosting live performances on the ground floor, along with a cafe and terrace, and a top-floor library and reading room, with exhibition spaces in between.

Locals sunbathe on the grassy fringes surrounding the building.

Exhibitions

Kiasma has no permanent displays; rather, exhibitions are mounted from its growing collection of more than 8500 works from more than 4000 Finnish and international artists.

Its ARS17+ exhibit covers changing displays of digital art, including mobile apps, blogs and social-media platforms. You can view it at the museum or online via Kiasma's website.

Kiasma for Kids

The museum is extremely family-friendly. Workshops for kids include a colour workshop for babies aged three months to 11 months, where infants can become acquainted with new colours and textures through seeing, touching, tasting, smelling and hearing. For ages five to eight, the 'Monster Route' has questions and activities such as colouring-in exercises over six stops (information is available in English).

Baby carriers can be borrowed for free from the cloakroom, and bottles can be warmed in the cafe's microwave.

Check before visiting as Kiasma's changing exhibitions may feature adult themes.

☑ Top Tips

▶ Guided tours in English lasting 45 minutes take place on the first Saturday of the month (included in admission).

▶ Sketching the artworks is encouraged; visitors can borrow a sketch board for free from the cloakroom. Bring your own paper and art supplies.

▶ Contemporary theatre productions are staged in the ground-floor theatre. Check the agenda for show times and ticket prices. Be aware that most productions are in Finnish and some feature nudity.

✗ Take a Break

Kiasma's sleek, glass-sided cafe and terrace are hugely popular with locals and visitors alike for modern Finnish bistro fare.

Some of Helsinki's best coffee, made from locally roasted beans, is brewed at nearby La Torrefazione (p34), which also serves pastries.

Top Sights
Kajsaniemi

Extensively replanted between 2012 and 2015, Helsinki's botanic gardens sprawl over 4 hectares adjacent to the north harbour, Töölönlahti, and are filled with plants from Finland and countries that share its latitude, with some 3600 species all up. Ten beautiful glass-paned interconnected greenhouses contain 800 species from across the globe and provide a wonderfully warm refuge when it's icy outside.

◉ Map p30, C2

www.luomus.fi

Kaisaniemenranta 2

gardens free, greenhouses adult/child €9/4.50

⏱ gardens 9am-8pm, greenhouses 10am-5pm Mon-Wed, Fri & Sat, to 6pm Thu, to 4pm Sun

History & Design

Finland's oldest scientific garden was founded in the former capital, Turku, in 1678. Following a devastating fire in 1829, when much of Turku was razed, the plants were relocated to this site, which was then a municipal park designed by CL Engel.

Head gardener of St Petersburg's botanic garden, Franz Faldermann, was commissioned to redesign the park to incorporate Turku's gardens. Faldermann's design resulted in the gardens' current layout of formal and informal sections. His main goal was to bring together native species from around Finland along with international species that would thrive beside them.

Most recently the gardens were given new life during renovations between 2012 and 2015, which saw the addition of a child-friendly sensory garden. Also here is an 1884-planted rockery garden and a rare plant garden.

Greenhouses

Kajsaniemi's grand greenhouses were designed by Finnish neo-Renaissance architect Gustaf Nyström in wrought iron and glass, and completed in 1832.

During the Continuation War (1941), the gardens were hit by three bombs and the greenhouses suffered extensive damage. All plants within them, with the exception of a single cypress and the seeds of a water lily, perished in the extreme cold.

Following the war, the greenhouses were rebuilt and later further restored. There are now 10 interconnected structures sheltering 800 species representing a cross-section of environments, including the African savannah and desert, Mediterranean forest, tropical palms and rainforest and South Pacific subtropical vegetation. The water lily in the rainforest greenhouse today is a direct descendant of the one that survived the war.

☑ Top Tips

▶ The greenhouses have a free cloakroom so you can lose your winter jacket when temperatures are frosty outside but a steamy 15°C to 25°C indoors.

▶ Picnicking is possible not only throughout the gardens, but also inside the greenhouses.

▶ In summer kids can get close to nature by running free on the sensory garden's barefoot trail, which incorporates different surfaces such as pine needles, gravel, sand, reeds and grass.

✗ Take a Break

Within the grounds, charming Café Viola, housed in a CL Engel–designed wooden building, serves dishes incorporating fruit, vegetables and herbs from the botanic gardens.

Just across Töölönlahti in Kallio, a beautiful 1897 timber boat is the home of Flying Dutch (p109), offering craft beers and ciders and outstanding gastropub fare.

Töölönlahti

A **B** **C** **D**

N 0 ———————— 200 m
0 ———————— 0.1 miles

1

For reviews see
- ◆ Top Sights p24
- ◉ Sights p31
- ✖ Eating p33
- 🍷 Drinking p34
- ⭐ Entertainment p35
- 🛍 Shopping p36

Gulf of Finland

Kaisaniemenranta

◉ *Kajsaniemi*

University Botanical Gardens

Kaisaniemenpuisto

2

✪ 11

Mannerheimintie

Mannerheiminaukio

3

◉ 2
Sanomatalo

Helsinki Train Station 🚉

Läntinen teatterikuja

KLUUVI

◉ 12

Mikonkatu

Kaisaniemi Ⓜ

Unioninkatu

Kiasma ◉

Elielinaukio

Postikatu

◉ 1
◉ *Rautatientori*

Rautatientori (Railway Square)

Vilhonkatu

Kaisaniemenkatu

Ⓜ Kaisaniemi

Lasipalatsi Centre

4

Kampintori (Kamppi Sq)

Ⓜ **Rautatientori**

Rautatientori Ⓜ

Kaivokatu

◉ *Ateneum*

Yliopistonkatu

✖ 7

Keskuskatu

Vuorikatu

Senaatintori (Senate Square)

Simonkatu

Yrjönkatu

13 🛍
9 🍷

Aleksanterinkatu

Kluuvikatu

Fabianinkatu

Helsinki City Tourist Office ℹ

🛍 18

Mannerheimintie

14 19
🛍🛍

Pohjoisesplanadi

10 🍷

✖ 4
6 16 17
🍷 🛍🛍 🛍 15
✖ 5

Esplanadin Puisto

8 🛍

5

Eerikinkatu

Annankatu

Kalevankatu

Lönnrotinkatu

◉ 3

Eteläesplanadi

Lönnrotinpuistikko

KEKYALYAYNEN/SHUTTERSTOCK ©

Rautatientori

Sights

Rautatientori SQUARE

 1 Map p30, C3

Rautatientori (Railway Sq) flanks the eastern side of Helsinki's glorious National Romantic art nouveau **train station** (Rautatieasema; www.vr.fi; Kaivokatu 1). Designed by Finnish architect Eliel Saarinen (1873–1950), the railway station is one of the world's most beautiful, with a granite facade, clock tower, copper roofing and twin pairs of statues holding spherical lamps that are illuminated when darkness falls. The Jääpuisto (p33) outdoor ice-skating rink sets up here in winter.

Sanomatalo NOTABLE BUILDING

2 Map p30, B3

The gleaming glass headquarters of the main daily newspaper, *Helsingin Sanomat,* is an iconic modern Helsinki building, designed by Finnish architects Jan Söderlund and Antti-Matti Siikala and completed in 1999. (Töölönlahdenkatu 2)

Esplanadin Puisto PARK

3 Map p30, D5

Locally known as 'Espa', oblong-shaped Esplanadi stretches for four blocks between the squares Erottaja to the west and the kauppatori to the east. Designed by architect CL Engel and

Understand

The Golden Age of Art

Finland's 'golden age' of art is the National Romantic era in the late 19th and early 20th centuries. The main features of these artworks are virgin forests and pastoral landscapes. Comprehensive collections are displayed at the Ateneum.

Fanny Churberg (1845–92) One of the most famous female painters in Finland, she created works using ahead-of-her-time techniques.

Albert Edelfelt (1854–1905) Educated in Paris. Many paintings are photo-like depictions of rural life.

Akseli Gallen-Kallela (1865–1931) An important figure in the National Romantic movement, drinking companion of composer Jean Sibelius and perhaps Finland's most famous painter. Had a distinguished and prolific career as creator of *Kalevala*-inspired paintings.

Pekka Halonen (1865–1933) Regarded a 'nature mystic', his work is mostly devoted to ethereal winter landscapes, is largely privately owned.

Eero Järnefelt (1863–1937) A keen visitor to Koli, where he created more than 50 paintings of the 'national landscape'. His sister married Sibelius.

Juho Rissanen (1873–1950) Depicted life among ordinary Finns, and his much-loved paintings are displayed at the Ateneum.

Tyko Sallinen (1879–1955) The greatest of the Finnish expressionists, Sallinen is often considered the last of the golden-age artists.

Helene Schjerfbeck (1862–1946) Probably the most famous female painter of her age, her self-portraits reflect life for Finnish women more than 100 years ago. Widely considered Finland's greatest artist.

Hugo Simberg (1873–1917) Most famous for his haunting work in Tampere's cathedral, which employs his characteristic folk symbolism. Also well represented in Helsinki's Ateneum.

Von Wright, Magnus (1805–68), **Wilhelm** (1810–87) and **Ferdinand** (1822–1902) The brothers von Wright are considered the first Finnish painters of the golden age, most famous for their paintings of birds.

Emil Wickström (1864–1942) Was to sculpture what Gallen-Kallela was to painting; he sculpted the memorial to Elias Lönnrot in Helsinki.

opened in 1818, it's one of the city's most loved green spaces and fills with picnickers on sunny days. Elegant shops, cafes and restaurants line the streets Pohjoisesplanadi (North Esplanadi) and Eteläesplanadi (South Esplanadi). At the park's eastern end is a bandstand out the front of grand cafe Kappeli (p34).

In the centre of the park is a **statue of Johan Ludvig Runeberg**, Finland's national poet and composer of the national anthem, which was unveiled in 1885.

Eating

Karl Fazer Café

CAFE **$**

4 Map p30, D5

Founded in 1891 and fronted by a striking art deco facade, this cavernous cafe is the flagship for Fazer's chocolate empire. The glass cupola reflects sound, so locals say it's a bad place to gossip. It's ideal, however, for buying dazzling confectionery, fresh bread, salmon or shrimp sandwiches, or digging into towering sundaes or spectacular cakes. Gluten-free dishes are available. (www.fazer.fi; Kluuvikatu 3; dishes €4-12; ☺7.30am-10pm Mon-Fri, 9am-10pm Sat, 10am-6pm Sun; 🛜🍴👶)

Strindberg

BISTRO **$$**

5 Map p30, C5

Strindberg has a casual ground-floor cafe and late-opening bar, but its finest dining is one flight up. In a

light-filled room overlooking leafy Esplanadin Puisto (p31), it serves dishes such as seared scallops with tomato risotto and basil foam, lamb sirloin with smoked black salsify, and pan-fried liver with creamed chanterelles, followed by lush desserts like raspberry pavlova with mascarpone mousse. (☎09-6128-6900; www.strindberg.fi; Pohjoisesplanadi 33; mains €21-31.50; ☺11am-10pm Mon-Sat)

Emo

EUROPEAN **$$$**

6 Map p30, C5

Popular with business diners, classy Emo serves dishes such as crab cakes with coriander and fennel, salt-baked trout with herb and juniper berry salad, halibut with wild garlic crème, and duck with red cabbage and apple in an elegant dining room decorated in sedate sage-green and oyster-grey hues. Astutely chosen wine pairings are available to complement each course. (☎010-505-0900; www.emo-ravintola.fi; Kluuvikatu 2; 3-course lunch

Local Life

Ice Skating on the Jääpuisto

In the winter months, Rautatientori (Railway Sq) transforms into a picture-book-like vision when skaters twirl on the **Jääpuisto** (Map p30, C3; Ice Park; ☎040-775-5791; www.icepark.fi; Rautatientori; adult/child €6/3, skate rental €6; ☺2-9pm Mon-Fri, 10am-9pm Sat & Sun Nov–Mar) outdoor ice rink.

menu €39, 4-/6-course dinner menus €54/69; ⏱11.30am-3pm & 5-10pm Mon-Fri, 2-10pm Sat, bar to midnight Mon-Sat)

Kanniston Leipomo
BAKERY $

7 Map p30, C4

Spectacular breads such as sourdough and rye are the hallmark of this fabulous Helsinki bakery chain, with half-a-dozen outlets around town. Alternatively, choose from savoury pastries such as a *karjalanpiirakka* (rice-filled rye Karelian pastry) or *lahapasteija* (cheese and sausage roll), or sweet options such as a *korvapuusti* (cinnamon scroll) or *vadelmapulla* (raspberry bun). There's a handful of seats inside. (www.kannistonleipomo. fi; Yliopistonkatu 7; pastries €2.50-4.50; ⏱7.30am-6pm Mon-Fri)

Local Life

La Torrefazione

Climb a flight of stairs to queue with locals getting their caffeine fix at **La Torrefazione** (Map p30, C5; www. latorre.fi; Aleksanterinkatu 50; ⏱7.30am-8pm Mon-Fri, 9am-7pm Sat, 10am-6.30pm Sun), which brews beans roasted in Helsinki to its own exacting specifications. La Torrefazione is so dedicated to its cause that it doesn't have wi-fi so you can focus solely on the coffee. It sources beans and creates roasting profiles for beans that are roasted in Helsinki, and prepares them using filter and drip brewing methods.

Drinking

Kappeli
BAR

8 Map p30, D5

Dating from 1867, this grand bar-cafe opens to an outdoor terrace seating 350 people and has regular jazz, blues and folk music in the nearby bandstand in Esplanadin Puisto (p31) from May to August. Locals and visitors alike flock here on a sunny day.

Now used for private functions, its cellar was a speakeasy during Finland's prohibition era (1919 to 1932), and still has paintings on its walls that were given in lieu of payment from artists at the time. (www.kappeli.fi; Eteläesplanadi 1; ⏱10am-midnight; 🛜)

Raffaellon Terassi
BEER GARDEN

9 Map p30, C5

In the covered Wanha Kauppakuja laneway, off Aleksanterinkatu, this terrace, or 'tunnel' (it's locally dubbed 'Mummotunneli') has several bars that turn into a party scene once the restaurant terraces are done with serving food for the night. DJs and live bands rev the crowds up every night. On Friday and Saturday, there's a €10 cover after 9pm. (www.raflaamo.fi; Wanha Kauppakuja, Aleksanterinkatu 46; ⏱4pm-3am Wed-Sat May-Sep)

Teatteri
BAR, CLUB

10 Map p30, C5

Attracting an older, relaxed crowd, this stylish spot alongside Esplanadi

Kansallisteatteri (p36) and statue of writer Aleksis Kivi

has a lounge bar, a cocktail bar with drinks themed for countries around the world and a sophisticated, strobe-lit nightclub (10pm to 4am Thursday to Saturday). Its pavement terrace swells in summer. (www.teatteri.fi; Pohjoisesplanadi 2; ☉9am-1am Mon & Tue, to 2am Wed, to 4am Thu & Fri, 11am-4am Sat, noon-10pm Sun)

Entertainment

Musiikkitalo
CONCERT VENUE

11 ⭐ Map p30, A2

Home to the Helsinki Philharmonic Orchestra, Finnish Radio Symphony Orchestra and Sibelius Academy, the glass- and copper-fronted Helsinki Music Centre, opened in 2011, hosts a diverse program of classical, jazz, folk, pop and rock. The 1704-capacity main auditorium, visible from the foyer, has stunning acoustics. Five smaller halls seat 140 to 400. Buy tickets at the door or from www. ticketmaster.fi.

The bar is a stylish place to hang out over a drink. There's an excellent classical-music store here. Check the online agenda for regular guided tours (English available; free to €14.50). (Helsinki Music Centre; ☎020-707-0400; www. musiikkitalo.fi; Mannerheimintie 13; tickets free-€30)

RICHARD l'ANSON/GETTY IMAGES ©

Kappeli (p34)

Kansallisteatteri

THEATRE

12 ⭐ Map p30, C3

The Finnish National Theatre was founded in 1872 as the country's first Finnish-speaking theatre, but didn't move into its permanent home until 1902. The beautiful art nouveau building was designed by architect Onni Törnqvist-Tarjanne, with a granite facade and interior of marble, soapstone and wood, and capacity for 1424 people. Performances are usually in Finnish; book tickets online through www.lippu.fi. (☏010-733-1331; www.kansallisteatteri.fi; Läntinen teatterikuja 1)

Shopping

Tre

DESIGN

13 🔒 Map p30, C4

If you only have time to visit one design store in Helsinki, this 2016-opened emporium is a brilliant bet. Showcasing the works of Finnish designers in fashion, jewellery and accessories, including umbrellas, furniture, ceramics, textiles, stationery and art, it also stocks a superb range of architecture and design books to fuel inspiration. (www.worldoftre.com; Mikonkatu 6; ⏱11am-7pm Mon-Fri, to 6pm Sat)

Artek

DESIGN

14 🔒 Map p30, C5

Originally founded by architects and designers Alvar Aalto and his wife Aino Aalto in 1935, this iconic Finnish company maintains the simple design principle of its founders. Textiles, lighting and furniture are among its homewares. Many items are only available at this 700-sq-metre, two-storey space. (www.artek.fi; Keskuskatu 1B; ⏱10am-7pm Mon-Fri, to 6pm Sat)

littala

DESIGN

15 🔒 Map p30, D5

Finland's famous glass manufacturer – established in 1881 in the southern Finnish town of the same name and later shaped by Alvar Aalto – has a central outlet here on Pohjoisesplanadi, and an outlet at Arabiakeskus (p129), 5km north of the city, which has a museum covering the brand. Along with glassware, it now creates ceramic, wood and textile designs. (www.iittala.com; Pohjoisesplanadi 25; 10am-8pm Mon-Fri, to 4pm Sat & Sun)

Aarikka
DESIGN

16 🔒 Map p30, D5

Specialising in wood, Aarikka was founded in 1954 and, along with furniture and homewares, is known for its distinctly Finnish jewellery. All of its designs are handcrafted in Finland. (www.aarikka.com; Pohjoisesplanadi 27; 10am-7pm Mon-Fri, to 5pm Sat, noon-5pm Sun)

Kalevala Koru
JEWELLERY

17 🔒 Map p30, D5

Gold, silver and bronze jewellery made by Kalevala Koru incorporates motifs based on Finnish history and legend. (www.kalevalakoru.fi; Pohjoisesplanadi 25-27; 10am-7pm Mon-Fri, to 5pm Sat)

Stockmann
DEPARTMENT STORE

18 🔒 Map p30, B5

Founded in 1862, Stockmann's 1930-built flagship store is Helsinki's biggest department store, spanning 50,000 sq metres. It carries luxury Finnish and international textiles, jewellery, fashion, cosmetics and much more, and has a large gourmet

food hall (www.info.stockmann.com; Aleksanterinkatu 52; 9am-9pm Mon-Fri, to 7pm Sat, noon-6pm Sun; 📶)

Akateeminen Kirjakauppa
BOOKS

19 🔒 Map p30, C5

Finland's biggest bookshop has a huge travel section, maps, Finnish literature and an impressively large English section, including magazines and newspapers. It's worth visiting alone just to view the striking modernist building, designed by Alvar Aalto and completed in 1969. The cafe here is named Cafe Aalto. (www.akateeminen.com; Pohjoisesplanadi 39; 9am-9pm Mon-Fri, to 7pm Sat, 11am-6pm Sun; 📶)

Explore

Kruununhaka & Katajanokka

Waterfront wraps around this maritime neighbourhood, which spans the Kruununhaka area – home to Helsinki's main market square, the kauppatori, where boats depart for cruises in summer – and the adjacent genteel island of Katajanokka, which is linked by bridges to the mainland and awash with National Romantic art nouveau architecture.

The Sights in a Day

Start your day at Helsinki's bustling market square, the **kauppatori** (p48), which is the city hub. From here, head to the Helsinki City Museum, **Helsingin Kaupunginmuseo** (p45), to learn about the city's history. Step inside CL Engel's magnificent neoclassical Lutheran cathedral, the **Tuomiokirkko** (p45). Close by is the **Uspenskin Katedraali** (p45), originally built as a Russian Orthodox church and now serving Finnish Orthodox worshippers. The two buildings face off high above the city like two queens on a theological chessboard.

After an exquisite lunch at **Olo** (p46), stroll through the elegant island of Katajanokka to appreciate the extravagant turrets and curious carvings of its National Romantic art nouveau architecture up close. Then loop back to the kauppatori to hop on an **archipelago cruise** (p46).

Finish up with a swim and/or sauna at the spectacularly sited **Allas Sea Pool** (p41), enjoying Nordic cuisine at its restaurant and unforgettable views over the city aboard the scenic Ferris wheel, the **Sky Wheel** (pictured, left; p46).

For a local's day in Kruununhaka and Katajanokka, see p40.

Local Life
Maritime Helsinki (p40)

Best of Kruununhaka & Katajanokka

Eating
Olo (p46)

Kolme Kruunua (p47)

Mumin Kaffe (p47)

Drinking
Johan & Nyström (p41)

Shopping
Lasikammari (p49)

Sweet Story (p49)

Getting There

🚋 **Tram** Trams 4 and 5 serve Katajanokka from the city centre; tram 5 continues north to Töölö. Line 7 from Kamppi cuts through Kruununhaka on its way north to Kallio.

⚓ **Ferry** From the kauppatori (market square), local ferries head to island destinations such as Suomenlinna and Helsinki Zoo.

Local Life
Maritime Helsinki

Helsinki is intrinsically linked with its maritime heritage, and this walk is never far from the water-front. It starts on an island that once served as a tar warehouse then takes in highlights including a light ship, more warehouses, the city's formidable icebreaker fleet and naval barracks before finishing at the harbour's passenger quays.

❶ Seaside Park

Named for the warehouses that safely stored flammable Finnish tar here prior to export, **Tervasaari** (Tar Island; Tervasaarenkannas) is now a landscaped park with spectacular views over Hel-sinki's skyline. Its wonderful summer restaurant, **Savu** (p46), specialising in smoked Finnish delicacies, is situated in the last remaining wooden tar storehouse.

❷ Lightship Libations

Built between 1886 and 1888, elegant old lightship **Majakkalaiva Relandersgrund** (www.majakkalaiva.fi; Pohjoisranta; ⏰noon-2am) was sunk by the Russians in 1918 and subsequently raised and repaired. The deck provides a fabulous venue for a coffee, beer or cider.

❸ Coffee by the Sea

A red-brick split-level harbourside warehouse with a waterside terrace is the atmospheric setting for this cafe run by boutique Swedish coffee roaster and tea merchant **Johan & Nyström** (Map p42, B3; www.johanoch nystrom.fi; Kanavaranta 7C; ⏰8am-7pm Mon-Sat, 9am-6pm Sun; 🛜).

❹ Break the Ice

Helsinki's **icebreaker fleet** (Merikasarmin laituri) is an impressively functional posse of around six heavy-duty ships. It's moored off the northern side of Katajanokka island.

❺ Naval Barracks

Architect CL Engel designed the **Merikasarmi** (Map p42, D3; Laivastokatu 22) naval barracks for the Russian military garrisoned here from 1816 to 1820 – the first of his many works in Helsinki. The neoclassical complex was home to the Finnish navy from Finnish independence in 1917 until 1968. Today it houses the Finnish ministry of foreign affairs and is closed to the public.

❻ Sea Swimming

Built from Finnish fir, swimming complex **Allas Sea Pool** (Map p42, B4; www.allasseapool.fi; Katajanokanlaituri 2; day ticket adult/child €12/6, towel rental €5; ⏰6.15am-11pm Mon-Fri, 8am-11pm Sat & Sun) sits right on the harbour against a spectacular city backdrop. It incorporates a bracing Baltic seawater pool, two freshwater pools (one for adults, one for kids; both heated to 27°C) and three saunas (male, female and mixed). Regular events include DJs or full-moon all-night nude swimming.

❼ Gone Fishing

Opened in 1896, Helsinki's oldest angling shop, **Schröder** (Map p42, A3; www.schroder.fi; Unioninkatu 23; ⏰10am-6pm Mon-Fri, to 4pm Sat), was the world's first to sell prized Rapala fishing lures – after Fritz Schröder met with Finnish designer Lauri Rapala prior to the 1952 Summer Olympics, Schröder sold them to international visitors, making them a household name. Today it still sells Rapala and other tackle, along with fishing licences and permits.

❽ Harbour Cruises

From Helsinki's main market square, the kauppatori, you can hop on a boat (p46) in summer to explore more of the city's maritime heritage.

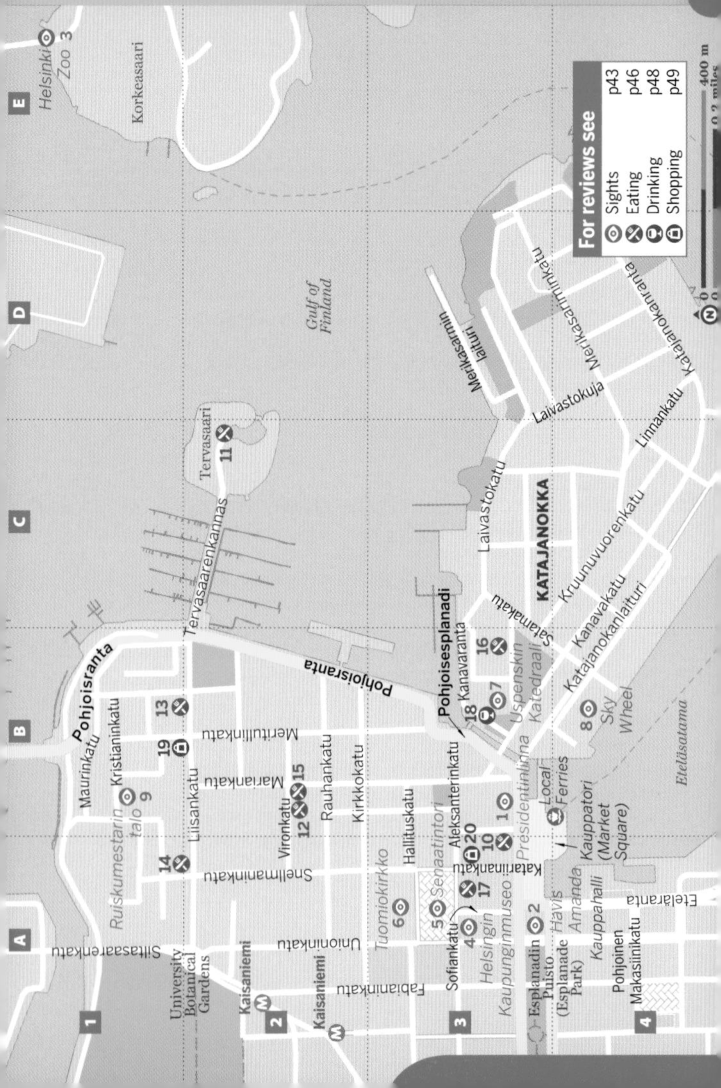

Helsinki
Zoo 3

Korkeasaari

For reviews see

Sights	p43
Eating	p46
Drinking	p48
Shopping	p49

400 m
0.2 miles

Gulf of
Finland

Tervasaari
11 ⊗

Tervasaarenkannas

Pohjoisranta

Pohjoisranta

Meritullintori

KATAJANOKKA

Kruunuvuorenkatu

Laivastokuja

Laivastokatu

Kanavakatu

Kanavaranta

Salmikatu

Katajanokanlaituri

Linnankatu

Katajanokanranta

Pohjoisesplanadi

16 ⊗

Uspenskin
Katedraali

18 ⊗ 7

Maurinkatu
Kristianinkatu
Ruiskumestarin
talo 9

19 ⊕

13 ⊗

Merttuilinkatu

Liisankatu

Mariankatu

Snellmaninkatu

12 ⊗ 15

Rauhankatu

Kirkkokatu

Hallituskatu

Aleksanterinkatu

Presidentinlinna

Local
Ferries

Sky
Wheel

8 ⊕

Etelasatama

14 ⊗

Unioninkatu

Kaisaniemi

University
Botanical
Gardens

Siltasaarenkatu

Kaisaniemi
M

Tuomiokirkko
6 ⊕

Sofiankatu

5 ⊕ 4 ⊕ Senaatintori
Helsingin
Kaupunginmuseo

17 ⊗ 20
1 ⊕ 10

Katariinankatu

Kauppatori
(Market
Square)

Esplanadin
Puisto
(Esplanade
Park)

Havis
Amanda

2 ⊕

Kauppahalli

Pohjoinen
Makasiinikatu

Fabianinkatu

Tuomiokirkko (p45)

Sights

Presidentinlinna PALACE

1 ◉ Map p42, B3

Overlooking the kauppatori, the striking neoclassical Presidentinlinna was designed by CL Engel and is one of the head of state's official residences. The interior is closed to the public. (Presidential Palace; www.presidentti.fi; Mariankatu 2)

Havis Amanda STATUE

2 ◉ Map p42, A3

Near the kauppatori, this bronze statue is the symbol of the city. Sculpted by Ville Vallgren in 1906 in Paris, and installed here in 1908, the nude female form's position on a pedestal, above splashing marine-creature fountains, initially attracted controversy, but is now widely admired.

Helsinki Zoo ZOO

3 ◉ Map p42, E1

Helsinki's leafy zoo occupies the entire island of Korkeasaari. Established in 1889 it has 150 animal species and 1000 plant species from Finland and around the world housed in large natural enclosures, as well as a tropical house, a small farm and a good cafe and terrace. Tickets are €2 cheaper from 4pm. In summer the most enjoyable way to travel here is by ferry from the kauppatori. Bus 16 runs from the

Understand

Capital of Independent Finland

From the 19th century, Helsinki grew rapidly and in 1816 German architect CL Engel was called on to dignify the city centre. Finland's first university, which had been founded in Turku in 1640, relocated to Helsinki in 1829. Between 1810 and 1890, Helsinki's population increased from 4000 to 60,000.

Finnish Nationalism

Stirrings of Finnish nationalism were being felt and academic studies of Finnish cultural traditions created a base on which future nationalistic feelings could be founded. Artists such as composer Jean Sibelius began to be inspired against the growing oppression, and the nation became emotionally ripe for independence. In 1904 the Russian Governor General of Finland, Nikolai Bobrikov, was assassinated by Finnish nationalist Eugen Schauman.

Declaration of Independence

In 1906 the Eduskunta parliament was introduced in Helsinki with universal and equal suffrage (Finland was the first country in Europe to grant women full political rights). The Russian Revolution of October 1917 enabled the Finnish parliament to declare the country's independence on 6 December of that year.

War & Peace

Following an attack by Russian-armed Finnish Reds on the civil guards in Vyborg, the Finnish Civil War flared in late January 1918. During 108 days of heavy fighting, approximately 30,000 Finns were killed. The Reds, comprising the rising working class, aspired to a Russian-style socialist revolution while retaining independence. The nationalist Whites, led by CGE Mannerheim, dreamed of monarchy and sought to emulate Germany.

The Whites, with substantial German help, eventually gained victory and the war ended in May 1918. Friedrich Karl, Prince of Hessen, was elected king of Finland by the Eduskunta on 9 October 1918, but the defeat of imperial Germany a month later made Finland choose a republican state model, under its first president, KJ Ståhlberg.

train station daily year-round. (www.
korkeasaari.fi; Mustikkamaanpolku 12, Korkeasaari; adult/child €16/8; ⊙10am-8pm May-Aug,
10am-4pm Oct-Mar, 10am-6pm Sep & Apr)

Helsingin Kaupunginmuseo

MUSEUM

 Map p42, A3

The Helsinki City Museum spreads
over five buildings from different eras,
including Sederholmin talo, Helsinki's
oldest central building (dating from
1757 and built by a wealthy merchant).
They're linked by a contemporary
structure, along with four other museums at separate locations. The must-
see of the bunch is the main museum.
Its collection of 450,000 historical
artefacts and over one million photographs is backed up by entertaining
information piecing together Helsinki's
transition from Swedish to Russian
hands and into independence. (Helsinki
City Museum; www.helsinginkaupunginmu-
seo.fi; Aleksanterinkatu 16; admission free;
⊙11am-7pm Mon-Fri, to 5pm Sat & Sun)

Senaatintori

SQUARE

5 Map p42, A3

From the kauppatori walk up the
cobbled Sofiankatu to Senaatintori
(Senate Sq), Helsinki's majestic
central square. Surrounded by early
19th-century buildings, the square
was modelled after St Petersburg's. CL
Engel's stately Tuomiokirkko, finished
in 1852, is the square's most prominent
feature and the steps are a favourite
meeting place.

Tuomiokirkko

CHURCH

6 Map p42, A3

One of CL Engel's finest creations,
the chalk-white neoclassical Lutheran
cathedral presides over Senaatintori.
Created to serve as a reminder of
God's supremacy, its high flight of
stairs is now a popular meeting place.
Zinc statues of the 12 apostles guard
the city from the roof of the church.
The spartan, almost mausoleum-like
interior has little ornamentation under the lofty dome apart from an altar
painting and three stern statues of
Reformation heroes Luther, Melanch-
thon and Mikael Agricola. (Lutheran
Cathedral; www.helsinginseurakunnat.fi;
Unioninkatu 29; admission free; ⊙9am-
midnight Jun-Aug, to 6pm Sep-May)

Uspenskin Katedraali

CHURCH

7 Map p42, B3

The eye-catching red-brick Uspenski
Cathedral towers above Katajanokka
island. Built as a Russian Orthodox
church in 1868, it features classic
golden onion-topped domes and now
serves the Finnish Orthodox congregation. The high, square interior has a
lavish iconostasis with the Evangelists
flanking panels depicting the Last
Supper and the Ascension.

Orthodox services held at 6pm on
Saturday and 10am Sunday are worth
attending for the fabulous chorals
and candlelit atmosphere. (Uspenski
Cathedral; www.hos.fi/uspenskin-katedraali;
Kanavakatu 1; admission free; ⊙9.30am-4pm
Tue-Fri, 10am-3pm Sat, noon-3pm Sun)

Sky Wheel

FERRIS WHEEL

8 Map p42, B4

Rising above the harbour, this Ferris wheel offers a fantastic panorama over central Helsinki from a height of up to 40m during the 10-minute 'flight'. A truly unique experience is the **SkySauna gondola**, allowing you to sauna and sightsee simultaneously: one hour (up to four people €240 to €320) includes towels, drinks and use of a ground-level Jacuzzi and lounge. (www.skywheel.fi; Katajanokanlaituri 2; adult/child €12/9; ⏰10am-9pm Mon-Fri, to 10pm Sat, 11am-7pm Sun May-Oct, shorter hours Nov-Apr)

Ruiskumestarin talo

MUSEUM

9 Map p42, B1

Mustard-coloured Ruiskumestarin talo is central Helsinki's oldest wooden townhouse, built in 1818. The charming cottage, with hardwood floors, fireplaces and printed wallpaper, has

---

☑ Top Tip

Sightseeing Cruises

Numerous summer cruises leave from the kauppatori (p48). A 1½-hour jaunt costs around €20 to €25; dinner cruises, bus-and-boat combinations and sunset cruises are also available. Most boat trips go past Suomenlinna (p51) and weave between other islands. Cruises run from May to September, and there's rarely any need to book. Just turn up and pick the next departure.

---

been furnished as it would have been when it was the home of the middle-class Wickholm family, who owned the property from 1859 to 1896, with day-to-day items such as a butter churn. (Burgher's House; www.ruiskumestarintalo.fi; Kristianinkatu 12; admission free; ⏰11am-5pm Wed-Sun early Jun-early Jan)

Eating

Olo

FINNISH $$$

10 Map p42, A3

At the forefront of new Suomi cuisine, Michelin-starred Olo occupies a handsome 19th-century harbourside mansion. Its memorable degustation menus incorporate both the forage ethos and molecular gastronomy, and feature culinary jewels such as fennel-smoked salmon, herring with fermented cucumber, Åland lamb with blackcurrant leaves, juniper-marinated reindeer carpaccio, and Arctic crab with root celery. Book a few weeks ahead. (☎010-320-6250; www.olo-ravintola.fi; Pohjoisesplanadi 5; 4-course lunch menu €53, dinner tasting menus short/long from €79/109, with paired wines €173/255; ⏰6-11pm Tue-Sat Jun–mid-Aug, 11.30am-3pm & 6-11pm Tue-Fri, 6-11pm Sat mid-Aug–May)

Savu

FINNISH $$

11 Map p42, C2

Dating from 1805, a rust-red wooden warehouse that once stored tar on **Tervasaari** (Tar Island; Tervasaarenkannas) now contains this delightful beam-ceilinged summer restaurant, which reflects its heritage in unique creations such as pine-tar-infused ice cream. Pine tar, birch and alder are all used to smoke meat, fish and vegetables at its smokery. Leafy trees and umbrellas shade the terrace.

Menu highlights include birch-smoked vendace with wholegrain mustard potato salad, alder-smoked salmon with forest mushroom stew, and pine-tar-smoked pork ribs with slaw. (☏09-7425-5574; www.ravintolasavu. fi; Tervasaari; mains €20-26, 3-course menus €41-54; ⊗noon-11pm Mon-Sat, 1-6pm Sun late May-Aug, 6-11pm Tue-Sat Sep)

Ask GASTRONOMY $$$

 12 Map p42, B2

Small organic or biodynamic Finnish farms and foraged game, fish, forest mushrooms, herbs and berries provide the ingredients for Michelin-starred Ask's superb-value lunch menus and 16- to 20-course evening tasting menus. Delicious, exquisitely presented morsels might feature buckwheat and nettle, reindeer and hazelnut, pike-perch and tar butter, beetroot and wild duck or burbot and spruce. Book several weeks ahead. (☏040-581-8100; www.restaurantask.com; Vironkatu 8; 4-course lunch menu €49, tasting menu €98, with paired wines €178; ⊗6pm-midnight Wed & Thu, 11.30am-1pm & 6pm-midnight Fri & Sat)

Kolme Kruunua FINNISH $$

13 Map p42, B1

Well off the tourist trail, this unpretentious local in Kruununhaka offers no-frills Finnish dishes such as fried Baltic herring, sautéed reindeer or handmade malt pork sausages in a fabulously retro dining area – with stained-glass windows, jade-green carpeting and a curvilinear timber bar – that hasn't changed since the 1950s. (☏09-135-4172; www.kolmekruunua. fi; Liisankatu 5; mains €15-33; ⊗kitchen 4pm-midnight Mon-Sat, 2-11pm Sun)

Mumin Kaffe CAFE $

 14 Map p42, A1

A delight for families, this comic-adorned cafe is themed around the Moomins, the adorable creations of Helsinki-born author and illustrator Tove Jansson. Sandwiches, cakes, pastries and freshly squeezed juices are all served on authentic Moomin plates, cups and glasses. There's a kids' seating area for little diners and high chairs for infants. There's official Moomin merchandise, including books, for sale. (www.muminkaffe.com; Liisankatu 21; dishes €3.40-9.50; ⊗9am-7pm; 🛜 👶)

Anton & Anton DELI $

 15 Map p42, B2

For gourmet picnic ingredients, this light-filled deli with black-and-white chequerboard tiles is a must. Fresh food changes with the seasons – there's a fantastic selection of Finnish cheeses, birch-smoked salmon, reindeer yoghurt, berries, locally baked breads, crisps, crackers, jams, chutneys and sweets such as

Kauppatori

Markets, from food markets to flea markets, regularly set up on the kauppatori (market square) in the warmer months. Shops selling arts, crafts and gifts are located between the kauppatori and Senaatintori. A handful of specialist shops cluster in the small streets northeast of Senaatintori.

salmiakki (salty Finnish liquorice). Ready-to-eat dishes include salads, sandwiches, wraps and savoury pastries and crêpes. (www.antonanton.fi; Mariankatu 18; dishes €3-6.50; ⊘8am-8pm Mon-Fri, to 6pm Sat)

Bellevue
RUSSIAN $$

16 Map p42, B3

Opened in 1917, Bellevue is Helsinki's oldest Russian restaurant. Along with its signature pot-roasted bear (€55), it offers more standard choices, from *zakuska* (mixed starters) and a range of blini (vendace roe, wild mushroom) to chicken Kiev and roast pheasant with beetroot troika, and cranberry soup for dessert. The atmosphere is elegant and old-fashioned. (✆09-179-560; http://restaurantbellevue.com; Rahapajankatu 3; mains €20-30.50; ⊘11am-11pm Tue-Fri, 5-11pm Sat mid-Aug–mid-Jun, 5-11pm Tue-Sat mid-Jun–mid-Aug)

Savotta
FINNISH $$

17 Map p42, A3

Themey but good quality, this representation of a logger's mess hall fits a lot of specialities from around Finland into its short but authentic menu. Staff in traditional dress are happy to explain the dishes, which include excellent fish mixed starters and mains such as succulent slow-roasted lamb or Arctic char. Summer dining is a pleasure on the courtyard terrace. (✆09-7425-5588; www.ravintolasavotta.fi; Aleksanterinkatu 22; mains €22-38; ⊘11am-11pm Mon-Sat, 6-10pm Sun)

Drinking

Holiday
BAR

18 Map p42, B3

Even on the greyest Helsinki day, this colourful waterfront bar transports you to more tropical climes with vibrant rainforest wallpapers and plants such as palms, tropical-themed cocktails like frozen margaritas and mojitos (plus two dozen different gins) and a seafood menu that includes softshell crab. A small market often sets up out front in summer, along with ping-pong tables. (http://holiday-bar.fi; Kanavaranta 7; ⊘4-11pm Tue-Thu, to 2am Fri, noon-2am Sat; 🛜)

Kauppatori

Shopping

Lasikammari ANTIQUES

19 🔒 Map p42, B1

Vintage Finnish glassware from renowned brands such as Iittala, Nuutajärvi and Riihimäki, and individual designers such as Alvar Aalto and Tapio Wirkkala, make this tiny shop a diamond find for collectors. Along with glasses, you'll find vases, jugs, plates, bowls, light fittings and artistic sculptures. Prices are exceptionally reasonable; international shipping can be arranged on request. (www.lasikam mari.fi; Liisankatu 9; ⏱noon-5pm Tue, Wed & Thu, to 2pm Mon, Fri & Sat)

Sweet Story FOOD

20 🔒 Map p42, A3

Handmade caramels, liquorices (including a traditional Finnish variety with tar) and a rainbow of boiled sweets at this fantasy land are all organic and free from gluten, lactose and artificial colours and preservatives. Most are made at Sweet Story's own Helsinki workshop. There's also a handful of other specialities from Denmark, Lithuania and Austria. (www.sweetstory.fi; Katariinankatu 3; ⏱10am-6pm Tue-Fri, 11am-4pm Sat)

Top Sights
Suomenlinna

Getting There

🚢**Ferries** (www.hsl.fi; single/return €3.20/5. 15 min, up to 4 hourly) depart from kauppatori. **Waterbuses** (www.jt-line.fi; return €7) depart there in summer, making three stops on Suomenlinna (20 minutes).

A Unesco World Heritage site, Suomenlinna, the 'fortress of Finland', was built by the Swedes in the mid-18th century and is spectacularly set over a series of car-free islands linked by bridges. Ferries from central Helsinki make the scenic journey to Suomenlinna, where you can explore museums, former bunkers and fortress walls, as well as Finland's only remaining WWII submarine.

Exploring Suomenlinna

At Suomenlinna's main quay, the pink **Rantakasarmi** (Jetty Barracks) is one of the best-preserved

Russian-era buildings. Make it your first stop to view its small exhibition and visit the multilingual **tourist office** (☏029-533-8420; www.suomenlinna.fi; ⏱10am-6pm May-Sep, to 4pm Oct-Apr), with downloadable content for your phone.

From here a blue-signposted walking path connects the key attractions. You'll immediately see the distinctive church, **Suomenlinnan Kirkko** (www.helsinginkirkot.fi; ⏱noon-4pm Wed-Sun, plus Tue Jun-Aug). Built by the Russians in 1854, this landmark church originally had five onion domes. It served as a Russian Orthodox place of worship until the 1920s, when it became Lutheran. The interior is stark and unadorned. It's one of the few churches in the world to double as a lighthouse – the beacon was originally gaslight, but is now electric and still in use.

Suomenlinna's most atmospheric area, **Kustaanmiekka**, is at the end of the blue trail. Exploring the old bunkers, crumbling fortress walls and cannons gives you an insight into this fortress. The monumental King's Gate was built in 1753–54 as a two-storey fortress wall that had a double drawbridge and a stairway added. In summer you can get a water bus to Helsinki from here, saving the walk back to the main quay.

At around 5.15pm it's worth finding a spot on Suomenlinna to watch the enormous Baltic ferries pass through the narrow gap between islands.

Ehrensvärd-Museo

On the main island, Susisaari, the **Ehrensvärd-Museo** (www.suomenlinna.fi; adult/child €5/2; ⏱10am-5pm Jun-Aug, 11am-4pm May & Sep) was once the home of Augustin Ehrensvärd, who designed the fortress and later the official residence of the fort's commanders. An attractive 18th-century house, it holds numerous portraits, prints and models giving an insight into daily life on the is-

---

Sveaborg

www.suomenlinna.fi

☑Top Tips

▸ **Guided walking tours** (☏029-533-8420; www.suomenlinna.fi; Rantakasarmi; adult/child €11/4; ⏱up to 3 times daily Jun-Aug, 1.30pm Sat & Sun Sep-May), departing from the tourist office, are a great way to learn about the island.

▸ Suomenlinna is car-free; pedicab operator **Taksi Viapori** (☏050-358-4686; www.taksiviapori.fi; per ride €5.20, 20min Suomenlinna tour €30) will take you anywhere on the islands for a flat fee.

✖Take a Break

▸ Suomenlinna has some lovely grassy spots; bring a picnic in fine weather.

▸ Microbrewery Suomenlinnan Panimo (p125) has ciders and beers accompanied by fresh fish and game platters.

land. Ehrensvärd's elaborately martial tomb sits outside in the square.

Opposite, sailmakers and other workers have been building ships since the 1750s at the picturesque **Viaporin Telakka** shipyard, which is today used for the maintenance of wooden vessels.

Vesikko

Along the shore, the **Vesikko** (www.suomenlinna.fi; Suomenlinna; adult/child incl Suomenlinna-Museo €7/4; ⊙11am-6pm May-Sep) is the only WWII-era submarine remaining in Finland. It saw action against the Russians during the Finnish Winter War (1939) and the Continuation War (1941), and was responsible for sinking the Russian merchant ship *Vyborg*. It's fascinating to climb inside the cramped space and see how it all worked, accompanied by sound effects, including crew commands, running machinery and a torpedo attack. Needless to say, there's not much room to move.

Suomenlinna-Museo

A two-level museum covering the history of the fortress, the **Suomenlinna-Museo** (adult/child incl Vesikko €7/4; ⊙10am-6pm May-Sep, 10.30am-4.30pm Oct-Apr) is located by the bridge that links Susisaari and Iso Mustasaari. It's information heavy, but provides good background. Displays (with interpretative signs in English) include maps and scale models of ships and the fortress itself. A helpful 25-minute audiovisual display plays

every 30 minutes (with multilingual headphones, including an English option).

Sotamuseo Maneesi
On Iso Mustasaari is **Sotamuseo Maneesi** (www.sotamuseo.fi; adult/child €7/4; ⏰11am-6pm early May-Sep), which has a comprehensive overview of Finnish military hardware from bronze cannons to WWII artillery. Russian and German military equipment is also displayed, along with uniform-clad mannequins.

Lelumuseo
Nearby, a three-storey wooden cottage houses **Lelumuseo** (Toy Museum; www.lelu-museo.fi; adult/child €6/3; ⏰11am-6pm May-Sep), a delightful private collection of hundreds of dolls and nearly as many teddy bears, dating from the early 19th century to the early 1970s. There are wind-up toys, model aeroplanes and boats, and dolls' houses. Look out for cute Moomin figures from the works of Helsinki-born author and illustrator Tove Jansson. The cafe serves delicious home-baked cakes, ice creams and lots of colourful sweets.

Explore

Punavuori & Ullanlinna

A trove of shops displaying furniture, art, fashion, accessories and homewares fill Helsinki's world-famous Design District, which centres on hip Punavuori. To its south, the more residential area of Ullanlinna shelters some beautiful parks, while creative and recreational spaces continue to open in the southwest on and around the Hernesaari waterfront.

The Sights in a Day

Start off by visiting the **Design Museum** (p56) to get up to speed on Finnish design. If you purchase a combination ticket, you can then visit the adjacent **Museum of Finnish Architecture** (p62) far more cheaply than by paying two separate admission fees. Browse the surrounding shops in the **Design District** (p58) and have lunch at one of its slew of cafes and restaurants.

The **Sinebrychoffin Taide-museo** (p65) is a must for art aficionados. History buffs won't want to miss the **Mannerheim-Museo** (p64), the home of former president and Finnish Civil War victor Baron Gustav Mannerheim. In fine weather especially, the **Kaivopuisto** (p64) is a wonderful escape. Otherwise, the **Löyly Sauna** (p65) makes a great place to warm up.

In the evening, return to the Design District to hop between its craft-beer and cocktail bars.

For a local's day in Punavuori, see p58.

Top Sights
Design Museum (p56)

Local Life
Design District (p58)

Best of Punavuori & Ullanlinna

Eating
Vanha Kauppahalli (p65)

Savoy (p66)

Saaga (p67)

Demo (p66)

Story (p66)

Drinking
Kaivohuone (p72)

Birri (p72)

Kaffa Roastery (p71)

Liberty or Death (p73)

Birri (p72)

Getting There

🚊 **Tram** All trams in Punavuori and Ullanlinna serve the city centre. Lines 2 and 10 serve Ullanlinna from Kamppi and Töölö; line 3 serves Punavuori and Ullanlinna from Kallio. Line 1 serves Punavuori from Kamppi and Töölö, while line 6 serves Punavuori from Kallio.

Top Sights
Design Museum

Design buffs can trace the evolution of Finnish design at Helsinki's impressively comprehensive Design Museum. Anchoring the city's Design District, it covers pioneering designers through to modern-day innovators, hosts exceptional exhibitions and events, including a free summer pavilion, and contains one of the country's best design shops with books, homewares and other Finnish icons.

👁 Map p60, D2

www.designmuseum.fi

Korkeavuorenkatu 23

adult/child €10/free

🕑 11am-6pm Jun-Aug, 11am-8pm Tue, to 6pm Wed-Sun Sep-May

The Building

The Design Museum is housed in a neo-Gothic former school. Designed by Finnish architect Gustaf Nyström and completed in 1894, it has grandly proportioned staircases and hallways with gleaming black-and-white chequerboard tiling. The museum has occupied the building since 1978.

Collections & Exhibitions

More than 75,000 objects, 45,000 drawings and 125,000 photographs are held in the museum's collections.

Its permanent exhibition focuses on the history of Finnish design from 1873 to the present day. Highlights include glassware (1932) by Aino Aalto; a Paimio bent birch plywood chair (1932) by Alvar Aalto; a Domus chair (1946) by Ilmari Tapiovaara; a semi-spherical fibreglass Ball chair (also known as a 'globe chair'; 1963) by Eero Aarniio; plastic orange-handled Fiskars scissors (1967); textiles by Annika Rimala (famed for her striped T-shirts), who worked for Marimekko, known for its 1964 Unikko (poppy) print patterns; and contemporary ceramics by Pauliina Pöllänen.

Temporary exhibitions are also drawn from the collection and centre on various themes, such as *An Invitation of Tomorrow*, predicting future trends, or *Utopia Now*, covering 1950s to 1990s Finnish designs, such as Nokia phones.

In 2017 the museum launched its digital collection, allowing visitors to see pieces not physically displayed in the museum space online. The initiative also enables you to read up on more background on objects on display, and the biographies of more than 1000 Finnish designers on your own device while you're at the museum.

☑ **Top Tips**

▸ From June to August, 30-minute tours in English take place at 2pm on Saturday and are included in admission.

▸ Combination tickets with the nearby Museum of Finnish Architecture (p62) are fantastic value.

▸ In summer the Design Museum and Museum of Finnish Architecture share a pavilion built each year by students from collaborating universities. Admission to the summer pavilion is free (no ticket to either museum is required).

✗ Take a Break

For designer twists on Finnish cuisine, try the daytime contemporary dishes or evening 'sapas' (Finnish tapas), along with Finnish craft beers, at nearby Juuri (p68).

Juuri also runs the museum's on-site cafe, which serves freshly baked breads, pastries, pies, salads, locally roasted coffee and craft beers at the museum's premises.

Local Life
Design District

After viewing iconic Finnish designs in Helsinki's Design Museum, set out on a treasure hunt through the Design District's streets to buy some to take home (shipping can invariably be arranged). This walk takes you to neighbourhood favourites, stopping off at a designer cafe en route, before finishing at a design bookshop.

❶ Old Made New

The emphasis is on pieces from the 1920s, '30s and '60s at small but well-organised vintage-design specialist **Bisarri** (www.bisarri.fi; Tarkk' Ampujankatu 5; ☺noon-5.30pm Mon-Thu, to 3pm Sat).

❷ Hot Stuff

With white tiles, turquoise flooring, birch and willow light fittings and hanging pot plants, the aptly named **Kuuma** (Map p60, C3; Albertinkatu 6;

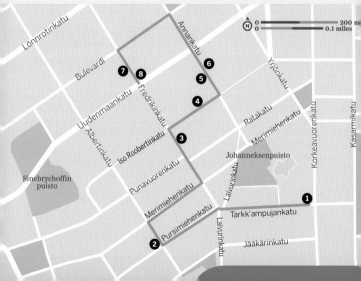

⏰8am-5pm Tue-Fri, 10am-4pm Sat; 🔊),
meaning 'hot' in Finnish, is a cafe
with an attached shop selling locally
made products from clothing to cosmetics, cushions and woolly blankets.

❸ Eco Design

At super-minimalist art gallery–
concept store **Awake** (www.awake-collec-
tive.com; Fredrikinkatu 25; ⏰12.30-6.30pm
Tue-Fri, 11am-4pm Sat), changing displays
of handmade Finnish designs range
from men's and women's fashion and
accessories to birch plywood furniture
and homewares such as rugs, carpets,
sheets and blankets. Everything is
ecologically and sustainably produced.
Regular evening art and fashion shows
are accompanied by champagne –
check the website for announcements.

❹ Glass House

Hand-blown and sculpted glass lamps,
vases, jewellery and kitchenware,
such as glasses, pitchers, mortars and
pestles, cooking bowls, salad bowls,
coasters and more, are created by
Marja Hepo-aho and Kari Alakoski
at their glass factory 70km north of
Helsinki (offering glass-making courses
in English on request). They're beautifully displayed here in their gallery-
boutique, **Mafka & Alakoski** (📞040-554-
9939; www.mafka-alakoski.fi; Iso Roobertinkatu
19; ⏰11am-6pm Tue-Fri, to 4pm Sat).

❺ Modern Magic

Treasure-filled **Art.fi** (www.art.fi; Annankatu 8; ⏰noon-5pm Mon-Fri) specialises
in 20th-century Finnish design (with
occasional forays into 18th- and 19th-
century folk art and antiques).

❻ Local Treasures

Hybrid design shop and gallery
Lokal (www.lokalhelsinki.com; Annankatu
9; ⏰11am-6pm Tue-Fri, 11am-4pm Sat, noon-
4pm Sun) has rotating exhibitions from
Finnish-based artists and designers,
including traditional woodcarver
Aimo Katajamäki, ceramicist Kristina
Riska, birch-bark painter and jeweller
Janna Syvänoja, contemporary painter
Visa Norros and industrial furniture
designer Jouko Kärkkäinen.

❼ Fancy Pants

Leading Finnish fashion designer **Jukka Rintala** (www.jukkarintala.fi; Fredrikinkatu
26; ⏰11am-6pm Mon-Fri, to 3pm Sat) is renowned for his women's evening wear,
which is often worn at presidential
functions and other high-profile events.
His talents also extend to jewellery, art
and interior design. Here you'll also
find prints of his artwork, jewellery
pieces and wallpaper designs.

❽ Book Nook

Glossy photo-filled books on Finnish
design, architecture, art, fashion,
music, photography and food are the
big draw of this airy, light-filled bookshop framed by full-length windows.
Nide (www.nidekauppa.fi; Fredrikinkatu
35; ⏰10am-7pm Mon-Fri, to 5pm Sat) also
stocks other nonfiction titles such as
philosophy books, fiction and periodi-
cals. Many titles are in English.

A   B   C   D

1

Laplinrinne

KAMPPI

Annankatu

Lönnrotinkatu

Eerikinkatu

Abrahaminkatu

Kalevankatu

Vanha
kirkkopuisto

Yrjönkatu

Rikhardinka

Bulevardi

19
18
17
32
21

Erottajankatu

Fredrikinkatu

37
39

9
26

Hietalahdenkatu

Uudenmaankatu

33

2

Lönnrotinkatu

Hietalahti
Flea Market
*Sinebrychoffin
Taidemuseo*

Bulevardi
6
12

28

36

34

35
25

Yrjönkatu

PUNAVUORI

41

Korkeavuorenkatu

*Desig
Museum*

Hietalahdenranta

Albertinkatu

Iso Roobertinkatu

Ratakatu

Annankatu

Laivurinkatu

Johanneksenpuisto

2

Johanneksenkirkk

3

Sinebrychoffin
puisto

Punavuorenkatu

Merimiehenkatu

31

40
22

Tarkk'ampujankatu

Jääkärinkatu

Laivurinkatu

38

Docksgatan
Telakkakatu

Pursimiehenkatu

Sepänkatu

Vuorimiehenkatu
24

Kapteeninkatu

27

4

EIRA

Telakkakatu

Ehrensvärdintie

Tehtaankatu

Armfeltintie

Laivurinkatu

Huvilakatu

Pietarinkat

Kapteeninkatu

5

Eiranranta

Eiranranta

Merikatu

Kaivopuisto

Merisatamanranta

E **Eteläesplanadi**

F

G

H

For reviews see
◎ Top Sights   p56
◉ Sights   p62
✖ Eating   p65
🍷 Drinking   p71
★ Entertainment p75
🔒 Shopping   p75

20 ✖

23 ✖   7 ✖
            11 ✖
Kauppahalli
         10 ✖
Pohjoinen Makasiinikatu
✖ 15

Kasarmikatu

Laivasillankatu

🚢 *Makasiiniterminaali*

Museum of Finnish Architecture

Eteläsatama

Observatory Hill Park
Tähtitorninvuoren puisto   3 ◉

Tähtitorninkatu

Vuorimiehenkatu

Laivasillankatu

🍷 *Olympia Terminaali*

Ehrenströmintie

Valkosaari

Luoto (Klippan)

ULLANLINNA

Tehtaankatu

Neitsytpolku   Pietarinkatu

Puistokatu

Kalliolinnantie
            4 ◉
Mannerheim-Museo

Iso Puistotie

Itäinen Puistotie

29 🍷

Merikatu

Kaivopuisto
5 ◉

Ehrenströmintie

Ehrenströmintie

✖ 14

Gulf of Finland

🍷 30

Sights

Museum of Finnish Architecture
MUSEUM

1 Map p60, E2

Finland's architecture museum occupies a neo-Rennaisance building dating from 1899. Exhibitions are its key focus, including the fascinating *Decades of Finnish Architecture 1900–1970*, which runs until the end of 2020 and covers National Romanticism, classicism, functionalism and modernism, laying the groundwork for Finland's definitive 1970s works, as well as shorter retrospectives and thematic exhibitions. Permanent displays include architectural models, drawings and photographs. There's a library and an excellent bookshop. The combination ticket with Helsinki's Design Museum (p56) is fantastic value.

In summer, there's also a shared summer pavilion between the two museums, built by students from collaborating universities to create a sustainable structure, with free admission. Another summer highlight is the guided walking tours in English run by the architecture museum in July and August. At 10am from Thursday to Monday, two-hour tours of Helsinki (adult/child €10/5), start from Senaatintori (p45) and finish at Helsinki's 1919-built National Romantic (art nouveau) train station (p141).In the beautiful park Kaivopuisto (p64), the museum also has a wooden villa, which opens for events; check for updates. (Arkkitehtuurimuseo; ☑045-7731-0474; www.mfa.fi; Kasarmikatu 24; adult/child €10/free, combination ticket with Design Museum €12/free; ☺11am-6pm Tue & Thu-Sun, to 8pm Wed)

Johanneksenkirkko
CHURCH

2 Map p60, D3

Helsinki's largest church, with seating for 2600 worshippers, is the soaring neo-Gothic St John's Lutheran Church. Designed by Swedish architect Adolf Melander, it's topped by distinctive 74m-high twin spires. Construction began in 1888; it was consecrated in 1891. Excellent acoustics make it a memorable place for free organ concerts at 7pm on Wednesdays in August, as well as ticketed concerts throughout the year – check the agenda online. (St John's Church; www.helsinginkirkot.fi; Korkeavuorenkatu 12; ☺10am-3pm Mon-Fri)

Observatory Hill Park
PARK

3 Map p60, F3

Designed in 1868 by Swedish landscaper Knut Forsberg in the style of a German city park, and completed in 1889 by his compatriot Svante Olsson, this sloping, 6.7-hectare park was created around its namesake **observatory** (Helsingin Observatorio; www.helsinki.fi; adult/child €8/4; ☺noon-8pm Thu, to 4pm Fri-Sun). The observatory ceased operating in 2010, but today houses an astronomy-focused exhibition space. Fires were once lit on the high, barren hill to guide seafarers into Helsinki's

Understand

Alvar Aalto

Alvar Aalto was for many the 20th century's number-one architect. In an era of increasing urbanisation, postwar rebuilding and immense housing pressure, Aalto found elegant solutions for public and private edifices that embraced functionalism but never at the expense of humanity. Viewed from the next century, his work still more than holds its own, and his huge contributions in other areas of art and design make him a mighty figure indeed.

Idealism

Aalto had a democratic, practical view of his field: he saw his task as 'a question of making architecture serve the wellbeing and prosperity of millions of citizens' where it had previously been the preserve of a wealthy few. But he was no utilitarian; beauty was always a concern, and he was adamant that a proper studio environment was essential for the creativity of the architect to flower.

Accomplishments

Born in 1898 in Kuortane, near Seinäjoki, Aalto worked in Jyväskylä, Turku and Helsinki before gaining an international reputation for his pavilions at the World Fairs of the late 1930s. His 1925 marriage to Aino Marsio created a dynamic team that pushed boundaries in several fields, including glassware and furniture design. Their work on bending and laminating wood revolutionised the furniture industry, and the classic forms they produced for their company, Artek, are still Finnish staples. Aalto's use of rod-shaped ceramic tiles, undulated wood, woven cane, brick and marble was particularly distinctive.

Aalto Buildings

Aalto's work is scattered across the country and all around Helsinki. In Punavuori is the renowned restaurant Savoy (p66), while the esteemed bookstore Akateeminen Kirjakauppa (p37) is across the way in the City Centre. Highlights in Kamppi include Finlandia Talo (p96) and the restaurant Kosmos (p91).

Johanneksenkirkko (p62)

harbour. Its grassy expanses, planted with tulips and daffodils, are especially picturesque in spring. (Tähtitorninvuoren puisto; Tähtitorninkatu)

Mannerheim-Museo

MUSEUM

4 ⊙ Map p60, G4

This fascinating museum by Kaivopuisto was the home of Baron Gustav Mannerheim, former president, commander in chief of the Finnish army and Finnish Civil War victor. The great field marshal never owned the building; he rented it from chocolate magnate Karl Fazer until his death. The house tells of Mannerheim's intrepid life with hundreds of military medals and photographs from his Asian expedition. Entry includes an informative, compulsory one-hour guided tour (in English); the last is at 3pm. (☏09-635-443; www.mannerheim-museo.fi; Kalliolinnantie 14; adult/child €12/ free; ⊙11am-4pm Fri-Sun)

Kaivopuisto

PARK

5 ⊙ Map p60, F5

On the waterfront, this sprawling park dating from 1834 is a favourite Helsinki idyll. There are expanses of lawns; numerous sculptures and winding paths; the waterside Mattolaituri (p73) cafe; a bar-club, Kaivohuone (p72) –

originally the park's spa, dating from 1838; and a small, domed observatory, **Ursa** (Kaivopuisto tähtitorni; ☎09-684-0400; www.ursa.fi; Kaivopuisto; adult/child €4/2; ⏱1-3pm Sun mid-Mar–mid-Jun, Aug & Sep, 7-9pm Tue-Sun mid-Oct–mid-Dec & mid-Jan–mid-Mar), dating from 1926. In winter, tobogganing down the slopes is a popular pastime for kids. Locals flock to the park on **Vappu** (May Day; ⏱1 May) for picnics with sparkling wine. (Puistokatu)

Sinebrychoffin Taidemuseo

GALLERY

6 ◉ Map p60, B2

One of Helsinki's finest collections of classic European paintings is in these 1842-built former brewery offices, which also contained living quarters for the Sinebrychoff family of brewers. On the 2nd floor, the house museum of Paul and Fanny Sinebrychoff displays the main collection of old masters, furniture and other artefacts bequeathed to the Finnish government by Fanny Sinebrychoff in 1921. The Empire room is an impressive re-creation that drips with chandeliers and opulence. Outstanding temporary exhibitions also take place here. (Sinebrychoff Art Museum; www.sinebrychoffintaidemuseo.fi; Bulevardi 40; house museum free, exhibitions adult/child €12/free; ⏱11am-6pm Tue, Thu & Fri, to 8pm Wed, 10am-5pm Sat & Sun)

Eating

Vanha Kauppahalli

MARKET **$**

7 ✗ Map p60, F1

Alongside the harbour, this is Helsinki's iconic market hall. Built in 1888 it's still a traditional Finnish market, with wooden stalls selling local flavours such as liquorice, Finnish cheeses, smoked salmon and herring, berries, forest mushrooms and herbs. Its centrepiece is its superb cafe,

Local Life

Löyly Sauna

In the emerging Hernesaari area, **Löyly Sauna** (☎09-6128-6550; www.loylyhelsinki.fi; Hernesaarenranta 4; per 2hr incl towel €19; ⏱4-10pm Mon, 1-10pm Tue, Wed & Sun, 7.30am-9.30am & 1-10pm Thu, 1-11pm Fri, 7.30am-9.30am & 1-11pm Sat) draws a loyal local crowd steaming in its saunas, splashing in the sea (and chilly winter ice hole) and dining on delicious specialities such as salmon soup at its panoramic glass-encased restaurant. Built from striking natural timbers in 2016, with a pine exterior made from 4000 custom-cut planks and a Scandinavian birch interior, Löyly is entirely powered by water and wind. Its two electric saunas and traditional smoke sauna offer direct access to the Hernesaari waterfront (and winter ice hole). All saunas are mixed and swimsuits are required (swimsuit rental costs €6).

Story. Look out too for soups from Soppakeittiö. (www.vanhakauppa halli.fi; Eteläranta 1; ☺8am-6pm Mon-Sat, plus 10am-5pm Sun Jun-Aug; ☒)

Savoy
FINNISH $$$

8 ✕ Map p60, E1

Designed by Alvar and Aino Aalto in 1937, this is one of Helsinki's grandest dining rooms, with birch walls and ceilings and some of the city's finest views. The food is a modern Nordic tour de force, with the 'forage' ethos strewing flowers and berries across plates that bear the finest Finnish game, fish and meat. (☎09-6128-5300; www.ravintolasavoy.fi; Eteläesplanadi 14; mains €37-44, 3-course lunch menu €63; ☺11.30am-3pm & 6pm-midnight Mon-Fri, 6pm-midnight Sat)

Demo
FINNISH $$$

9 ✕ Map p60, C1

Book to get a table at this chic Michelin-starred spot, where young chefs wow with modern Finnish cuisine. Artfully presented, daily changing combinations are innovative (blackcurrant and liquorice-leaf marinated Åland lamb, spruce-smoked pumpkin with chanterelles, king crab with nettle pesto and vendace roe) and the slick contemporary decor appropriate: this is a place to be seen, not for quiet contemplation.

From June to mid-August, it also runs a fabulous outdoor kitchen at Mattolaituri (p73) in Kaivopuisto. (☎09-2289-0840; www.restaurantdemo.

fi; Uudenmaankatu 9; 4-/5-/6-/7-course menus €62/75/92/102, with paired wines €110/138/170/185; ☺4-11pm Tue-Sat)

Story
CAFE $

10 ✕ Map p60, F1

At the heart of Helsinki's historic harbourside market hall Vanha Kauppahalli, this sparkling cafe sources its produce from the surrounding stalls. Breakfast (oven-baked barley porridge, eggs Benedict) gives way to snacks (cinnamon buns, cakes) and hearty mains such as creamy salmon and fennel soup, aubergine ragout with couscous, and shrimp-laden *skagen* (Swedish-style open-faced sandwiches). Its outdoor terrace overlooks the water. (www.restaurantstory.fi; Vanha Kauppahalli, Eteläranta; snacks €3.20-10, mains €12.80-17; ☺kitchen 8am-3pm Mon-Fri, to 5pm Sat, bar to 6pm Mon-Sat; ☒)

Soppakeittiö
SOUP $

11 ✕ Map p60, F1

A great place to warm the cockles in winter, this soup stall inside the Vanha Kauppahalli is renowned for its bouillabaisse, which is almost always on the menu. Other options might include cauliflower and goat's cheese, smoked reindeer or potato and parsnip. There are also branches at the Hietalahden Kauppahalli (p92) in Kamppi, and Hakaniemen Kauppahalli (p110) in Kallio. (www.sopakeittio.fi; Vanha Kauppahalli; soups €9-10; ☺11am-5pm Mon-Sat; ☒)

Vanha Kauppahalli (p65)

Saaga

FINNISH $$

12 Map p60, B2

Chandeliers made from reindeer antlers and split-log benches lined with reindeer furs adorn this rustic timber-lined Lappish restaurant. Specialities from Finland's far north include char-grilled whitefish with sour milk sauce and roast elk with juniper berry sauce, followed by desserts such as Lappish squeaky cheese with sea buckthorn cream or liquorice cake with birch ice cream and cloudberries. (☎09-7425-5544; www.ravintolasaaga.fi; Bulevardi 34; mains €22-27, 3-course menus €49-65; ☺6-11pm Mon-Fri late May-Aug, 6-11pm Mon-Sat Sep & Oct)

Saslik

RUSSIAN $$

13 Map p60, E3

Screened by tasselled curtains, Saslik's succession of aristocratic dining rooms have stained-glass windows, gilt-framed paintings of Russian hunting scenes and flowing tablecloths. *Borscht* (sour beetroot soup), lamb *pelmeni* (dumplings made from un-leavened dough), blini with aubergine and black caviar, and potted-bear stroganoff are among its specialities, along with desserts such as baked Alaska. Traditional Russian musicians often perform. (☎09-7425-5500; www.ravintolasaslik.fi; Neitsytpolku 12; mains €24-37, 3-course menus €49-65; ☺6-11pm

Mon-Fri, noon-11pm Sat Sep-Jul, 6-11pm
Tue-Sat Aug)

Café Ursula

CAFE **$$**

14 Map p60, G5

Offering majestic views over the
Helsinki archipelago, this upmarket
cafe has marvellous outside summer
seating. In winter you can sit in the
modern interior and watch the ice
on the sea. Along with daily specials,
dishes range from elaborate open
sandwiches to portobello burgers with
goat's cheese and sweet-potato fries
to Russian-style bavette steaks and
grilled Baltic herring.

Sunday brunch (€32) is a local
event. In summer the bar opens until
midnight. (www.ursula.fi; Ehrenströmintie
3; lunch buffet €10.50, mains lunch €11-17,
dinner €17.50-28.50; ⏲9am-9pm Mon & Tue,
to 10pm Wed-Sat, to 8pm Sun; 🛜)

The Cock

PUB FOOD **$$**

15 Map p60, E1

The Cock combines a free-wheeling
bar with ping-pong tables (hosting
regular tournaments) and brilliant
cocktails such as its house G&T
(with pink grapefruit, lingonberry
and Helsinki dry gin) and Blue Mule
(blueberry-infused vodka, fresh mint,
lime and ginger beer) with pub food
spanning organic beef tartare with
raw egg and bavette steak with Bé-
arnaise sauce to white-wine-steamed
mussels. (☑09-6128-5100; www.thecock.
fi; Fabianinkatu 17; mains lunch €12-22, dinner
€22-28; ⏲kitchen 11am-11pm Mon-Fri, noon-
11pm Sat, bar to late Mon-Sat; 🛜)

Juuri

FINNISH **$$**

16 Map p60, D2

Creative takes on classic Finnish
ingredients draw the crowds to this
stylish modern restaurant, but the
highlight here is sampling the 'sapas'
– tapas with a Suomi twist (€7.80 per
plate) – which is only served in the
evenings. You might graze on rhubarb-
marinated horse, juniper berry and
pork croquettes, spruce-smoked salm-
on, or herring with horseradish crème.
(☑09-635-732; www.juuri.fi; Korkeavuoren-
katu 27; mains €18-25; ⏲11.30am-2.30pm &
5-11pm Mon-Fri, noon-11pm Sat, 4-11pm Sun)

Grotesk

STEAK **$$$**

17 Map p60, D1

Elegant but reasonably informal, this
former bank has a Finnish-baroque
dining room where cured meat starters precede excellent meats grilled
on a Spanish Josper (charcoal oven),
accompanied by an especially good,
fairly priced wine list. The attached
bar is popular in summer when it
migrates into the sheltered courtyard
space with regular DJs. (☑010-470-
2100; www.grotesk.fi; Ludviginkatu 10; mains
€26-42; ⏲5-9pm Tue-Thu, to 10pm Fri & Sat,
bar to midnight; 🛜)

Gaijin

JAPANESE **$$**

18 Map p60, D1

With *toro* lanterns and *shoji* screens,
this sleek, dark timber-panelled
restaurant combines elegant Japanese
fare with other North Asian influ-
ences, including Korean and northern

Chinese. Intricate dishes (*saikyo-miso*-marinated roast salmon with asparagus and wasabi emulsion; crispy drunken chicken with black rice vinegar and roast chilli) are accompanied by craft cocktails such as Haiku (sake, aloe vera, yuzu and apple). (☎010-322-9386; www.gaijin.fi; Bulevardi 6; mains €24-32; ⏲5-10.30pm Mon & Sat, 11.30am-2pm & 5-10.30pm Tue-Fri, 5-10pm Sun, dinner only early Jul-early Aug)

Ragu
ITALIAN $$

19 Map p60, D1

Braised beef tongue with roast pecorino, seared scallops with pike and lemon gnocchi, and whole roast cockerel with nettle risotto and smoked yoghurt are among the refined modern Italian dishes at this elegant restaurant, supported by a high-end, all-Italian wine list. Finish off with desserts such as liquorice panna cotta with marinated blood orange and Aperol sorbet. (☎09-596-659; www.ragu.fi; Ludviginkatu 3; mains €16-27; ⏲5-9.30pm Mon-Sat)

Zucchini
VEGETARIAN $

20 Map p60, E1

One of the city's original and most popular vegetarian cafes, Zucchini is a top-notch lunch spot; queues out the door aren't unusual. Steaming soups banish winter chills, while freshly baked quiche on the sunny terrace is a summer treat. Year-round you can choose soup or a salad/hot dish or both. At least one vegan dish features

on the daily changing menu. (Fabianinkatu 4; lunch mains €8-12; ⏲11am-4pm Mon-Fri; 🖋)

Skiffer
PIZZA $

21 Map p60, D1

Nautical-themed artworks brighten the low-lit interior of this out-of-the-ordinary pizza joint. Choices include the Hangö (juniper-berry-marinated herring and smoked whitefish) and Surf & Turf (crayfish and chorizo); smaller kids' pizzas are available for €10. It's a popular meeting spot, so be prepared to wait for a table. (www.skiffer.fi; Erottajankatu 11; pizzas €13-17.50;

MAHARA/SHUTTERSTOCK ©

Salmon soup

⏱11am-9pm Mon & Tue, to 10pm Wed & Thu, 1-11pm Fri & Sat, 1-8pm Sun; 📶👍)

Brooklyn Cafe

BAGELS $

 22 Map p60, C3

Bagels handmade by Brooklyn Cafe come in varieties such as sesame, onion, poppy seed and pumpkin seed, with fillings such as salt-cured salmon and chive cream cheese or prosciutto, mozzarella and black pepper as well as veggie and vegan options. It also bakes cupcakes and rich dark-chocolate brownies topped with vanilla ice cream and caramel sauce. (www.brooklyncafeandbakery.com; Fredrikinkatu 19; bagels €4.20-7.50; ⏱8.30am-6.30pm Mon-Fri, 9am-5.30pm Sat, 10.30am-5.30pm Sun Jun-Sep, shorter hours Oct-May; 📶📞)

Local Life

Konepahalli

Steel girders and pulleys still line the cavernous brick **Konepahalli** (Map p60, B4; Telakkakatu 6), dating from the early 20th century, which was formerly used for shipbuilding. Craft-beer bars, cafes and restaurants serving the likes of Vietnamese *pho* (noodle soup) and Caribbean cuisine, Finnish design shops and a gym now fill the hall. Outside, the concrete courtyard has a beer garden that hosts live gigs in summer.

Goodwin

STEAK $$$

 23 Map p60, E1

There's a lot to be said for doing one thing well, and Goodwin achieves it, with tenderised steaks cooked to order on a Josper (super-hot Spanish charcoal oven). Sides include Josper-grilled corn cobs and blue-cheese mash. Kids' menus cost between €8.50 and €10.50. The split-level space is done out in stylish timbers; look for the lounging cow statue out front. (📞050-419-8000; www.steak.fi; Eteläranta 14; mains €27-39; ⏱11am-11pm; 👍)

Sea Horse

FINNISH $$

 24 Map p60, D3

A seahorse mural takes up an entire wall of this traditional Finnish restaurant dating from the 1930s. Locals gather in the gloriously unchanged interior to meet and drink over hefty dishes of Baltic herring, Finnish meatballs, liver and cabbage rolls. (📞09-628-169; www.seahorse.fi; Kapteeninkatu 11; lunch buffet €10.30, mains €25-38; ⏱10.30am-10pm Mon-Fri, noon-10pm Sat & Sun)

Fafa's

FAST FOOD $

 25 Map p60, D2

A cut above the usual kebab places, everything at Fafa's is organic, with meat, vegetarian and vegan pitas, as well as salads (gluten-free breads are also available). There are 11 branches in all throughout Helsinki, including this one on Iso Roobertinkatu, which

View from Observatory Hill Park (p62)

stays open until the wee hours on weekends. (www.fafas.fi; Iso Roobertinkatu 2; dishes €10-12.50; ⊙11am-10pm Mon-Thu, to 5am Fri & Sat, noon-2am Sun; 🐾)

Café Bar 9   CAFE $

26 ✕ Map p60, D1

With retro red Formica tables, vinyl bar stools and an unpretentious, artsy air, this cafe is a good bet for inexpensive but filling dishes day and night, from big sandwiches, salads, pastas and burgers to steaks and Thai-inspired stir-fries in generous portions. (www.bar9.fi; Uudenmaankatu 9; mains €10-17; ⊙11am-11pm Mon-Fri, noon-11pm Sat & Sun; 🛜)

Drinking

Kaffa Roastery   COFFEE

27 ☕ Map p60, B4

Processing up to 4000kg of beans every week, this vast coffee roastery supplies cafes throughout Helsinki, Finland and beyond. You can watch the roasting in progress through the glass viewing windows while sipping Aeropress, syphon or V60 brews in its polished concrete surrounds. It also stocks a range of coffee grinders, espresso machines and gadgets. (www.kaffaroastery.fi; Pursimiehenkatu 29A; ⊙7.45am-6pm Mon-Fri, 10am-5pm Sat; 🛜)

Understand
New Directions in Finnish Design

A strong design tradition tends to produce good young designers, and Finland's education system is strong on fostering creativity, so Suomi is churning them out at a fair rate. New names, ranges and shops crop up in Helsinki's Design District like mushrooms overnight, and exciting contemporary design is being produced on all fronts. Fennofolk is the name for one broad movement that seeks, like the original giants of Finnish design, to take inspiration from Suomi's natural and cultural heritage, adding a typically Finnish injection of weirdness along the way.

There are exciting things continuing to happen across all fields of design. Paola Suhonen's IVANAhelsinki clothing label combines innovation with practicality and sustainability, while Hanna Sarén's clothing continues to go from strength to strength since being referenced in *Sex and the City*. Julia Lundsten and Minna Parikka are head-turning young stars of the footwear world.

In industrial design, Harri Koskinen is a giant; his clean-lined minimalism produces objects that are always reassuringly practical but quite unlike anything you've ever seen before. Helsinki bristles with high-quality graphic-design studios that are leading lights in their field.

Birri   MICROBREWERY

28 Map p60, C2

Birri brews three of its own beers on-site at any one time, stocks a fantastic range of Finnish-only craft beers and also handcrafts its own seasonally changing sausages. The space is strikingly done out with Arctic-white metro tiles, brown-and-white chequerboard floor tiles, exposed timber beams and gleaming silver kegs.

Weekend brunch (11am to 1.30pm Saturday, to 2pm Sunday) is among Helsinki's best. (Il Birrificio; http://ilbirri.fi; Fredrikinkatu 22; ⊙11am-11pm Mon-Thu, to 1am Fri & Sat, to 4pm Sun)

Kaivohuone   BAR, CLUB

29 Map p60, F4

Built in 1838 as a spa in the Kaivopuisto (p64) park, this pavilion was later remodelled in art deco style and has been fabulously restored with dazzling multicoloured chandeliers and opens to a vast terrace. Food is served until 4pm. DJs pack the club three nights weekly in summer. Minimum age is 20 on Wednesday and Friday, and 24 on Saturday. (☎020-775-9825; www.kaivohuone.fi; Iso Puistotie 1, Kaivopuisto; ⊙bar noon-midnight May-Aug, club 10pm-4am Wed, Fri & Sat May-Aug; 🛜)

Mattolaituri
BAR

30 · Map p60, F5

In Kaivopuisto (p64) park, this summer beach bar overlooking the sand and glittering sea is an idyllic spot to lounge in a deck chair or umbrella-shaded sofa with a coffee, glass of wine, or a cocktail. Live music plays most nights from 6pm from June to August. Michelin-starred restaurant Demo (p66) sets up an outdoor kitchen here from June to mid-August. (☎045-119-6631; Ehrenströmintie 3A, Kaivopuisto; ⏰9am-midnight May-Sep)

Bier-Bier
CRAFT BEER

32 · Map p60, D1

Inside a glorious high-ceilinged, timber-panelled former bank dating from 1893, this jewel of a bar has a serious drinks list, with over 100 different beers categorised by taste and provenance, along with a stellar selection of 20 ciders and 20 astutely chosen wines. Expert staff can guide you through the offerings. The small, supremely elegant space creates an intimate atmosphere. (www.bier-bier.fi; Erottajankatu 13; ⏰4pm-midnight Mon-Thu, 2pm-2am Fri & Sat)

Liberty or Death
COCKTAIL BAR

33 · Map p60, D2

Blacked-out windows make it easy to miss, but open the door and you'll find this small vintage-furnished speakeasy with exposed-brick walls lined with bookshelves. Made from rare spirits and seasonal fruit and herbs, each of its signature and classic cocktails, such as Hemingway's Moustache (Tullamore Dew, dry sherry, lavender and Galliano), comes with its own offbeat story. (www.libertyordeath. bar; Erottajankatu 5; ⏰6pm-1am Mon-Thu, to 2am Fri & Sat)

Tommyknocker Helsinki
CRAFT BEER

34 · Map p60, C2

Helsinki might be a long way from Tommyknocker Brewery in the small Colorado mountain town of Idaho Springs, but its medal-winning ales and lagers rotate on the taps at this Finnish outpost. There are eight at any one time, plus another 60 mostly American craft beers in bottles. Passionate staff can make recommendations. (www.tommyknocker.fi; Iso Roobertinkatu 13; ⏰2pm-2am Mon-Fri, noon-2am Sat, 2pm-midnight Sun)

TheRiff
BAR

35 · Map p60, D2

Signed guitars, drums and posters cover the walls of this rock 'n' roll bar, which functions as a before- and after-party for gigs around town for musicians and their fans. A soundtrack of hard rock and metal keep the crowds revved up. In summer the action spills out onto the terrace. (www.theriff.fi; Iso Roobertinkatu 3; ⏰2pm-3am)

Kaivopuisto (p64)

Andante

CAFE

36 Map p60, C2

Design District hang-out Andante is both a fragrant florist selling pot plants and bouquets of blooms and a cafe brewing organic, fair-trade coffee etched with intricate coffee art (oat milk available). There's also a wide range of Chinese teas, seasonal smoothies and juices, and snacks such as raw cakes with raspberry and goji berry or green tea and lingonberry. (Fredrikinkatu 20; ⌚noon-7pm Wed-Fri, 11am-6pm Sat & Sun; ☏)

Los Cojones

BAR

37 Map p60, C1

A lighthearted Spanish theme here is backed up by hanging hams, wine barrels, guitars and bullfighting posters. It's an atmospheric spot for a glass of wine or shot of oaky Jerez brandy and gets very lively later. You can soak it up with a range of *pintxos* (Basque tapas). (Annankatu 15; ⌚6pm-1am Mon & Tue, to 2am Wed & Thu, 4pm-3am Fri & Sat; ☏)

Entertainment

Nosturi
LIVE MUSIC

38 Map p60, B3

This atmospheric harbourside warehouse, with a capacity of 900, hosts regular concerts with known Finnish and international performers. Acts range from folk to hip-hop to metal. Book tickets on its website or at www.lippu.fi. (www.elmu.fi; Telakkakatu 8)

Shopping

Frank/ie
DESIGN

39 Map p60, C2

In addition to creating the products stocked at this shop, the designers also take turns in staffing it. Look out for shoes and accessories by Kuula + Jylhä; men's, women's and kids' fashion made from recycled and surplus materials by Kiks; jewellery and casual women's wear by Jatuli; and women's fashion utilising mixed fabrics and monochrome colours by Miia Halmesmaa. (www.frankie.fi; Annankatu 13; ⏱noon-6pm Tue-Fri, to 5pm Sat)

Roobertin Herkku
FOOD

40 Map p60, C3

Salmiakki (salty Finnish liquorices) in over two dozen different sizes, shapes, textures and flavours are among the dazzling kaleidoscope of sweets at this colourful shop, which was reopened in

Top Tip

Shop Till You Drop

If airline baggage restrictions mean you're travelling light, you don't need to confine yourself to window shopping in Helsinki's Design District: the profusion of shops here are able to arrange international shipping. Information about the district, including a map of shop locations, is available online at www.designdistrict.fi.

2014 by the granddaughter of the original 1963 founder. *Tervaleijona* (tar drops) are another Finnish speciality. There are also more conventional boiled sweets, chocolate-covered berries and lollipops. (www.roobertinherkku.fi; Fredrikinkatu 19; ⏱10am-8pm Mon-Fri, to 6pm Sat, noon-6pm Sun)

Domus Classica
HOMEWARES

41 Map p60, D2

The inspiration behind renovator's dream Domus Classica came when the owners were sourcing authentic materials for their conversion of a 1910 stable to a contemporary home. They now stock original vintage items such as door handles, tapware, tiles, lighting and fireplace grills, as well as brand-new fittings and fixtures made to their own designs. (www.domusclassica.com; Erottajankatu 11; ⏱10am-6pm Mon-Fri, 11am-4pm Sat, closed Sat Jul)

Explore

Kamppi & Töölö

Abutting the city centre to the west, lively Kamppi is a busy transport hub and home to outstanding museums and cultural institutions. To its north, peaceful Töölö is a lovely, leafy area that stretches to Hietaranta, one of Helsinki's most popular beaches.

The Sights in a Day

☀ Kamppi is right by the city centre, so it's an ideal place to kick off your explorations. The district is packed with museums: you'll have to make some choices. The headliners here are the **Kansallismuseo** (p78) and the **Tennispalatsi** (p80), housing the **Helsinki Art Museum** (p81), but other museums include the **Amos Andersonin Taidemuseo** (p88) and, from 2018, its vast new gallery space, the subterranean Amos Rex. Also in this compact area, take time to visit stunning churches, both historic – **Vanha Kirkko** (p86) – and new – **Kamppi Chapel** (pictured left; p88).

☀ Indulge in an exceptional and artistic lunch at **Grön** (p83). Afterwards, make your way to Töölö, which has another truly unique church, the rock-carved **Temppeliaukion Kirkko** (p89). If it's beach weather, stroll via the **Hietaniemi Cemetery** (p90) to sandy **Hietaranta** (p89).

☽ By night, the Alvar Aalto–designed **Finlandia Talo** (p96) is one of several superb entertainment venues. Alternatively, explore the district's edgier side with a tour of local nightlife (p82).

For a local's evening in Kamppi, see p82.

◎ Top Sights

Kansallismuseo (p78)

Tennispalatsi (p80)

◔ Local Life

Helsinki by Night (p82)

♥ Best of Kamppi & Töölö

Eating
Grön (p83)

Konstan Möljä (p93)

Kosmos (p91)

Drinking
Steam Hellsinki (p94)

A21 (p94)

Teerenpeli (p82)

Getting There

Ⓜ **Metro** The metro station is Inside the Kamppi bus station, with services to the city centre and Kallio.

🚊 **Tram** Trams 7 and 9 link southern Kamppi with the city centre and Kallio. Lines 1, 2, 4 and 10 travel Kamppi's northeastern edge to Töölö. Tram 8 travels along Kamppi's western edge north to Töölö then east to Kallio.

🚌 **Bus** Kamppi bus station (p141) services the northern suburbs and regional destinations.

Top Sights
Kansallismuseo

To learn how Finland has evolved over the millennia, a visit to the Kansallismuseo is a must. Inside a monumental National Romantic art nouveau building dating from 1916, the story of the country's history unfolds at its premier historical museum through archaeological finds, church relics, ethnography and changing cultural exhibitions.

The Building
Looking a bit like a Gothic church, with its heavy granite and steatite stonework and tall, square

National Museum of Finland

👁 Map p84, D5

www.kansallismuseo.fi

Mannerheimintie 34

adult/child €10/free, 4-6pm Fri free

🕙11am-6pm Tue-Sun

tower, the building housing the Kansallismuseo is one of Helsinki's most distinctive.

Helsinki architects Herman Gesellius, Armas Lindgren and Eliel Saarinen won a design competition in 1902 for their National Romantic art nouveau–style design, and construction took place from 1905 to 1910.

Its vaulted central hall leads to the museum's galleries. In the hall, look up to the ceiling to see the magnificent frescoes painted by Helsinki artist Akseli Gallen-Kallela with scenes from Finland's national epic, the *Kalevala*. Gallen-Kallela based the frescoes on the ones he painted in the Finland pavilion at Paris' Exposition Universelle (World Fair) in 1900.

The Collections

A major update of the museum's permanent exhibitions is ongoing until 2019, but the museum will remain open throughout, with few disruptions for visitors. When complete, Finland's **Museum of Cultures**, which holds ethnographic collections from all continents, will also be permanently housed here.

Already updated at the time of writing, the **prehistory exhibition**, covering the last ice age to the end of the Iron Age, takes you back in time to experience Finland 10,000 years ago. You can handle an axe made from reindeer bone, watch a mammoth move and animate a cave painting. Finds from around Finland include animal motifs, weapons and jewellery.

Also already updated, **the Realm**, covering the 13th to 19th centuries, explores the country's history under Catholic and Lutheran church rule, Swedish secular rule and Finland's annexation by the Russian Empire.

☑ **Top Tips**

▶ Admission to the museum is free on Friday from 4pm to 6pm.

▶ In July and August, 30-minute guided tours in English at 11.30am from Tuesday to Friday are included in admission.

▶ Kids will love Workshop Vintii, where they can get involved in hands-on activities such as harnessing a horse, building a log cabin or sitting on a throne and contemplating ruling the land.

✗ **Take a Break**

The museum's on-site cafe has sweet and savoury snacks, but for a wider range of dishes (including great filled rolls) and drinks, head to Tin Tin Tango (p93).

Soak up the historic surrounds of Carelia (p92), set in a former pharmacy with original timber cabinets, which serves well-prepared brasserie fare as well as excellent wines.

◉ Top Sights
Tennispalatsi

Completed in 1938, the cultural and recreation centre Tennispalatsi was intended for the 1940 Summer Olympics, which were cancelled following the outbreak of WWII. Today the freshly renovated complex is best known as the home of the superb Helsinki Art Museum (HAM), but it also contains a cinema, cafes, restaurants and speciality shops.

The Building
Occupying an entire city block, this vast complex was designed by Helsinki architect Helge Lund-

Tennis Palace

◉ Map p84, D6

Eteläinen Rautatiekatu

ström in functionalist style for the 1940 Olympics. It was never used for its intended purpose due to the onset of WWII.

Plans to tear down the structure were abandoned in 1990 when its architectural and historic value were recognised. The Helsinki Art Museum (HAM) and FinnKino Tennispalatsi cinema moved into the complex in 1999. Following extensive renovations, its latest incarnation, with increased gallery space and facilities, was unveiled in 2015.

Helsinki Art Museum

Helsinki's **contemporary art museum** (HAM; www. hamhelsinki.fi; Eteläinen Rautatiekatu 8; adult/child €10/ free; ⏰11am-7pm Tue-Sun), most commonly known as HAM, oversees 9000 works, including 3500 city-wide public artworks. The overwhelming majority of its 20th- and 21st-century works are by Finnish artists; it also presents rotating exhibitions by emerging artists in its 3000-sq-metre gallery space.

Exhibitions last for seven weeks, so you never know what you'll encounter; check the online agenda for a heads-up.

HAM Metro

If you have a valid public-transport ticket (www. hsl.fi), head to the lower floor of the Kamppi metro station to find HAM Metro – an exhibition space with vividly coloured street-art murals and sculpture exhibits.

Cinema

New-release films are shown at the **FinnKino Tennispalatsi** (www.finnkino.fi; Salomonkatu 15; tickets adult/child €11.50/9.20) cinema inside the complex, which has 14 screens. Most films are in English.

☑ Top Tips

▶ The Helsinki Art Museum always has at least one free exhibition that doesn't require a ticket to the museum's main section.

▶ On the last Saturday of the month at 3pm, guided tours of the Helsinki Art Museum, lasting 30 to 40 minutes depending on the exhibitions, are included in admission.

✖ Take a Break

The Tennispalatsi complex has half-a-dozen cafes, restaurants and fast-food outlets (such as a branch of Hesburger, Finland's answer to McDonald's). The pick of the bunch is Lumière, serving French brasserie fare.

Two blocks east of the Tennispalatsi, sip ales, stouts or berry ciders at Teerenpeli (p82), which has its microbrewery in Lahti in Finland's Häme region.

Local Life
Helsinki by Night

Finland's buzzing capital doesn't hibernate after dark. Delve into the city's nightlife on this evening walk, starting with a Finnish craft beer or berry cider, popping into an incongruously peaceful chapel, then plunging back into the scene with a round of neon-lit minigolf, a drink at a rock bar and more.

① Craft Beer

In a long, split-level space with romantic low lighting and intimate tables, excellent pub **Teerenpeli** (www.teerenpeli.com; Olavinkatu 2; ☺noon-2am Mon-Thu, to 3am Fri & Sat, to midnight Sun; 🛜) serves superb ales, stouts and berry ciders from its microbrewery in Lahti. There's a minimum age limit of 20.

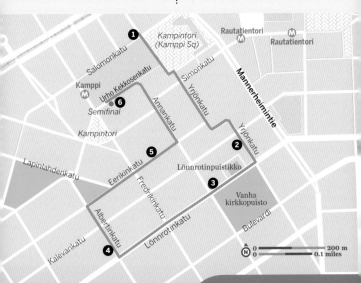

❷ Minigolf

Finland is crazy about minigolf, and indoor complex **Hohtogolf** (☎09-2519-1112; www.hohtogolf.fi; Yrjönkatu 24; adult/child per round €14/10; ☺4-9pm Mon & Tue, 2-9pm Wed & Thu, noon-11pm Fri & Sat) takes it to another level with a range of glow-in-the-dark courses with themes such as a carnival, the tropics, sports and zombies. You can also go curling (on synthetic ice), or head into the laser maze. There's an on-site bar. From 8pm on Friday and Saturday, the minimum age is 18.

❸ Rock Bar

The scarlet-coloured interior seems too stylish for a rock bar, but that's what **Bar Loose** (www.barloose.com; Annankatu 21; ☺8pm-4am Wed-Sat, 11pm-4am Sun; 🛜) is, with portraits of guitar heroes lining one wall and an eclectic crowd upstairs, served by two bars. Downstairs is a club area, with live music more nights than not and DJs spinning everything from metal to mod/retro classics.

❹ Fine Dining

Finnish artists not only provide the dining room's ceramic plates and paintings on the whitewashed walls at exceptional bistro **Grön** (☎050-328-9181; www.restaurantgron.com; Albertinkatu 36; mains €23-26, 4-course menu €49; ☺5-10pm Tue-Sat; 🛜🍴), but also forage for the kitchen's wild herbs, berries and mushrooms, and catch its fish. There are just 20 seats, so book ahead.

❺ Cool Bar

The offbeat film-making Kaurismäki brothers designed and once owned drinking den **Corona Baari** (www.andorra.fi; Eerikinkatu 11-15; ☺Corona 11am-2am Mon-Thu, to 3am Fri & Sat, noon-2am Sun, Kafe Mockba 6pm-2am Mon-Thu, to 3am Fri & Sat; 🛜). It has pool tables, no door person, an island bar and a relaxed mix of people.

❻ Live Rock

One of Helsinki's legendary rock venues, **Tavastia** (☎09-7746-7420; www.tavastiaklubi.fi; Urho Kekkosenkatu 4; ☺8pm-1am Sun-Thu, to 3am Fri, to 4am Sat) attracts both up-and-coming local acts and bigger international groups, with a band virtually every night of the week. Most gigs start at 9pm; doors open two hours beforehand. New talent and young local bands take the stage at its adjoining venue, **Semifinal** (Map p84, D7; ☎09-7746-7420; www.tavastiaklubi.fi; Urho Kekkosenkatu 6; ☺8pm-1am Sun-Thu, 9pm-2am Fri, 8pm-4am Sat).

KALLIO

Ensi linja

Eläintarhantie

Töölönlahti

☆ 34

For reviews see
◆ Top Sights   p78
⊙ Sights   p86
✕ Eating   p90
⊙ Drinking   p94
✪ Entertainment p96
🛈 Shopping   p99

500 m
0.25 miles

🧭 N

Helsinginkatu

Kaupunginpuutarha

Mäntymäentie

39 ✪

Mannerheimintie

Töölönkatu

17 ✕

Runeberginkatu

13 ✕

Töölöntori

20 ✕

Pohjoinen Hesperiankatu

Hesperiankatu

Apollonkatu

City
Winter
Gardens

Pohjoinen
Stadiontie

11 ⊙

Olympic
Stadium

38 ✪

Finnair
Stadium

37 ⊙

Urheilukatu

Savonkatu

Mannerheimintie

Ratikkamuseo
10 ⊙
Eino Leinonkatu

Sibeliuksenkatu

Topeliuksenkatu

Nordenskiöldinkatu

Topeliuksenkatu

Mechelininkatu

Sibelius
Park

Sibelius
Monument
8 ⊙

Merikannontie

12 ✕

Stenbäckinkatu

Linnankoskenkatu

Pacuiuksenkatu

Helsinki Train Station

Kansallismuseo

TÖÖLÖ

Töölönlahdenkatu

Rautatientori

Mannerheimintie

See Enlargement

PUNAVUORI

Iso Roobertinkatu

Johanneksenpuisto

Ratakatu

Vanha Kirkko

Annankatu

Vanha kirkkopuisto

Uudenmaankatu

Fredrikinkatu

Albertinkatu

Sinebrychoffin puisto

Lönnrotinkatu

Bulevardi

Parliament House

Luonnontieteellinen Museo

Museo

Kamppi (Kampp Sq)

Kamppi Kamppi Chapel

Kamppi Bus Station

Kampintori

KAMPPI

Yrjönkatu

Runeberginkatu

Kalevankatu

Eerikinkatu

Malminkatu

Lapinlahdenkatu

Arkadiankatu

Nervanderinkatu

Museokatu

Tennispalatsi

Temppelikatu

Temppeliaukion Kirkko

Runeberginkatu

Mechelinkatu

Hietaniemenkatu

Ruoholahdenkatu

Hietalahdenranta

Heitakannaksentie

Hietaniemi Cemetery

Hietaniemi Cemetery

Hietaniemenkatu

Seurasaarenselkä

Hietaranrarua

Mannerheimintie

Amos Andersonin Taidemuseo

Yrjönkadun Uimahalli

Yrjönkatu

Kalevankatu

Yrjönkatu

100 m
0.05 miles

0
0

KIEV.VICTOR/SHUTTERSTOCK ©

Interior of Kamppi Chapel (p88), designed by K2S Architects Ltd

Sights

Vanha Kirkko

CHURCH

1 ◉ Map p84, E7

Helsinki's most venerable church is this white wood 1826 beauty, designed by CL Engel. Opposite the church is a **memorial to Elias Lönnrot** (Lönnrotin-puistikko, Lönnrotinkatu), compiler of the *Kalevala* epic. (www.helsinginkirkot.fi; Lönnrotinkatu 6; ◷noon-3pm Mon-Wed & Fri, to 8.30pm Thu)

Yrjönkadun Uimahalli

SWIMMING

2 ◉ Map p84, B7

For a sauna and swim, these art deco baths are a Helsinki institution – a fusion of soaring Nordic elegance and Roman tradition. There are separate hours for men and women. Nudity is compulsory in the saunas; bathing suits are optional in the pool. Bring your own towel or rent one for €4. (www.hel.fi; Yrjönkatu 21B; adult/child swimming €5.50/2.50, swimming plus saunas €14/7; ◷men 6.30am-8pm Tue & Thu, 7am-8pm Sat, women noon-8pm Sun & Mon, 6.30am-8pm Wed & Fri, closed Jun-Aug)

Understand

Finland's National Epic

It's hard to overestimate the influence on Finland of the *Kalevala,* an epic tale compiled from the songs of bards that tells everything from the history of the world to how to make decent home brew. Intrepid country doctor Elias Lönnrot trekked eastern Finland during the first half of the 19th century in order to collect traditional poems, oral runes, legends, lore and folk stories. Over 11 long tours, he compiled this material with his own writing to form what came to be regarded as the national epic of Finland.

Story Lines

The mythology of the book blends creation stories, wedding poems and classic struggles between good and evil. Although there are heroes and villains, there are also more nuanced characters that are not so simply described. The main storyline concentrates on the events in two imaginary countries, Kalevala (characterised as 'our country') and Pohjola ('the other place', or the north). Many commentators feel that the epic echoes ancient territorial conflicts between the Finns and the Sámi. Although impossible to accurately reproduce the Finnish original, the memorable characters are particularly well brought to life in poet Keith Bosley's English translation of the *Kalevala,* which is a fantastic, lyrical read.

Evolution & Inspiration

The first version of the *Kalevala* appeared in 1833, with another following in 1835 and yet another, the final version, *Uusi-Kalevala* (New Kalevala), in 1849. Its influence on generations of Finnish artists, writers and composers was and is immense, particularly on painter Akseli Gallen-Kallela and composer Jean Sibelius, who repeatedly returned to the work for inspiration.

Beyond Finland the epic has influenced the Estonian epic *Kalevipoeg* and American poet Henry Wadsworth Longfellow. Indeed, JRR Tolkien based significant parts of his mythos on the *Kalevala*.

Across from the Vanha Kirkko (p86) is a memorial to Elias Lönnrot, compiler of the *Kalevala* epic, depicting the author flanked by his most famous character, 'steady old Väinämöinen'.

TELIA/SHUTTERSTOCK ©

Parliament House

Amos Andersonin Taidemuseo

GALLERY

3 ◎ Map p84, A7

This gallery occupies the 1913 apartment building built for publishing magnate Amos Anderson (1878–1961), one of the wealthiest Finns of his time. As well as housing modern art from his collection and temporary exhibitions that mix the old and cutting-edge contemporary, you can view the Empire-style interiors of Anderson's home as well as his private chapel. The museum is also opening a vast new space, the subterranean Amos Rex, 300m north on Lasipalatsinaukio in mid-2018. (www.amosander son.fi; Yrjönkatu 27; adult/child €10/free; ⊙10am-6pm Mon, Thu & Fri, to 8pm Wed, 11am-5pm Sat & Sun)

Kamppi Chapel

CHAPEL

4 ◎ Map p84, D6

Built in 2012 by Helsinki architectural firm K2S, this exquisite, ultra-contemporary curvilinear chapel is constructed entirely from wood (wax-treated spruce outside, oiled alder planks inside, with pews crafted from ash) and offers a moment of quiet contemplation in cocoon-like surrounds. Its altar cross is the work of blacksmith Antti Nieminen. Known as the Chapel of Silence, the Lutheran chapel is ecumenical and welcomes people of all faiths (or none). (www.helsinginseurakunnat.fi; Simonkatu 7; ⏰8am-8pm Mon-Fri, 10am-6pm Sat & Sun)

Luonnontieteellinen Museo MUSEUM

5 ◉ Map p84, D6

The city's natural history museum is known for its controversial weathervane of a sperm impregnating an ovum. Modern exhibitions such as *Story of the Bones,* which puts skeletons in an evolutionary context, bring new life to the University of Helsinki's extensive collection of mammals, birds and other creatures, including all Finnish species. Download the free audio app from the website.

Admission is free on the first Friday of the month, from 2pm to 5pm June to August, and from 1pm to 4pm from September to May. (Natural History Museum; www.luomus.fi; Pohjoinen Rautatiekatu 13; adult/child €13/6; ⏰10am-5pm Tue, Wed & Fri-Sun, to 6pm Thu Jun-Aug, 9am-4pm Tue, Wed & Fri, to 8pm Thu, 10am-5pm Sat, 10am-4pm Sun Sep-May)

Parliament House NOTABLE BUILDING

6 ◉ Map p84, D5

Finland's imposing parliament building was designed by Finnish architect Johan Sigfrid Sirén and inaugurated in 1931. Its pared-back neoclassicism combined with early 20th-century modernism gives it a serious, even somewhat mausoleum-like appearance. After lengthy renovations of its facade and interior (including a total replacement of its utilities) as part of Finland's centenary of independence commemorations, it reopened in 2017. It's possible to visit by guided tour (English tours are available); check the website for details. (Eduskunta; 📞09-432-2199; www.eduskunta.fi; Mannerheimintie 30)

Temppeliaukion Kirkko CHURCH

7 ◉ Map p84, C5

Hewn into solid stone, the Temppeliaukio church, designed by Timo and Tuomo Suomalainen in 1969, feels close to a Finnish ideal of spirituality in nature – you could be in a rocky glade were it not for the stunning 24km-diameter roof covered in 22km of copper stripping. Its acoustics are exceptional; regular concerts take place here. Opening times vary depending on events, so phone or search for its

Local Life
Hietaranta

Helsinki has several city beaches, but Hietaranta is considered the best. In summer the golden sands are beloved by locals soaking up the sunshine, swimming in the chilly waters, paddling canoes and SUPs and grilling sausages by nearby Cafe Regatta (p90). The nicest way to get here is to stroll from Mechelininkatu west through the Hietaniemi cemetery (p90).

Facebook page updates. There are fewer groups midweek.

A short prayer is offered in English at noon on Monday, Tuesday, Thursday and Friday. (📞09-2340-6320; www.helsinginseurakunnat.fi; Lutherinkatu 3; adult/child €3/free; ⏱9.30am-5.30pm Mon-Thu & Sat, to 8pm Fri, noon-5pm Sun Jun-Aug, shorter hours Sep-May)

Sibelius Monument   MONUMENT

 8 Map p84, B3

In the leafy, waterfront Sibelius Park (Sibeliuksen puisto, or just 'Sibban'), this famous, striking sculpture was created by artist Eila Hiltunen in 1967 to honour Finland's most famous composer. Its 600 steel pipes evoke a sound wave in their formation. Bus 24 runs here, but it's a pleasant walk or cycle. (Mechelininkatu)

Hietaniemi Cemetery   CEMETERY

9 Map p84, B5

Famous Finns buried at this sprawling 1829-established cemetery include architect Alvar Aalto and military leader and statesman Carl Gustav Emil Mannerheim, along with numerous artists and fallen war heroes. (www.helsinginseurakunnat.fi; Hietaniemenkatu; ⏱7am-10pm)

Ratikkamuseo   MUSEUM

 10 Map p84, C2

Transport enthusiasts and kids will especially enjoy checking out the vin-tage trams at this engaging museum, which depicts daily life in Helsinki's streets in past decades, beginning with the inception of horse-pulled trams in 1891. Look out for family-friendly events such as concerts, art exhibitions and theatre performances. (Tram Museum; 📞09-3103-6630; www.trammuseum.fi; Töölönkatu 51A; admission free; ⏱11am-5pm)

Olympic Stadium   STADIUM

 11 Map p84, C1

Host of the 1952 Summer Olympics, this still-attractive functionalist stadium is a city landmark. The complex is closed for major renovations and will reopen in 2019. (Paavo Nurmen tie)

Eating

Cafe Regatta   CAFE $

 12 Map p84, B3

In a marvellous waterside location, this historic rust-red wooden cottage is scarcely bigger than a sauna, but has great outdoor seating on the bay. You can hire a canoe or paddleboards alongside, buy sausages and grill them over the open fire, or just kick back with a drink or *korvapuusti* (cinnamon scroll). Expect to queue on sunny weekends. Cash only. (www.caferegatta.fi; Merikannontie 10; dishes €1.50-5; ⏱8am-10.30pm)

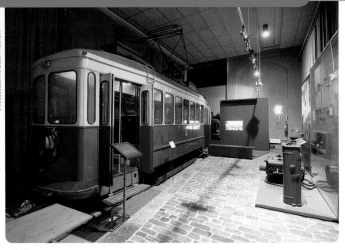

Ratikkamuseo

Kuu

FINNISH $$

13 Map p84, C3

Traditional Finnish fare is given a sharp, contemporary twist at Kuu, which creates dishes from local ingredients such as smoked reindeer heart with pickled forest mushrooms, poached pike-perch with Lappish fingerling potatoes, and liquorice ice cream with cloudberry soup. Wines aren't cheap, but there are some interesting choices. Its casual bistro sibling, KuuKuu, is located 800m south. (☎09-2709-0973; www.ravintolakuu. fi; Töölönkatu 27; mains €19-30, 2-/3-course lunch menus €24/28, 4-course dinner menus €47-51; ⏰11.30am-midnight Mon-Fri, 2pm-midnight Sat, 4-11pm Sun)

Kosmos

FINNISH $$

14 Map p84, B7

Designed by Alvar Aalto, this 1924-opened restaurant is a Helsinki treasure, with a traditionally Finnish atmosphere and classic dishes such as reindeer, sweetbreads, kidneys and fish, along with amazing rye bread made from a 1940s starter. Service is impeccable. (☎09-647-255; www.kosmos.fi; Kalevankatu 3; mains €16-32; ⏰11.30am-11pm Mon-Fri, 4-11pm Sat, bar to 1am)

Hietalahden Kauppahalli

MARKET $

15 🍴 Map p84, D8

Dating from 1903 and beautifully restored, this red-brick indoor market at Hietalahti has charming wooden food stalls and eateries, including enticing cafes with upstairs seating at each end. A flea market sets up here in the summer months. (www.hietalahdenkauppahalli.fi; Lönnrotinkatu 34; ⏰8am-6pm Mon-Thu, to 10pm Fri & Sat, 10am-4pm Sun; 🍴)

Kitch

CAFE $

16 🍴 Map p84, A8

With big picture windows, this laid-back space is great for watching the world go by. Furnished with recycled materials, it offers generous tapas portions (such as roasted beetroot with goats cheese), original salads (including a fantastic crab Caesar salad) and fat burgers (chicken and avocado; barbecue with apple and fennel slaw). Produce is primarily sustainably sourced. (www.kitch.fi; Yrjönkatu 30; mains €14.50-17, tapas €3.50-6; ⏰11am-10pm Mon & Tue, to 11pm Wed-Sat mid-Aug–mid-Jun, 3-11pm Tue-Fri, noon-11pm Sat mid-Jun–mid-Aug; 🛜🍴)

Carelia

BRASSERIE $$

17 🍴 Map p84, C3

In a former pharmacy, this striking spot opposite the Oopperatalo is ideal for a pre- or post-show drink or meal. Glamorously decorated in period style, with original timber cabinetry, it offers smart brasserie fare (pork fillet with beetroot and tar sauce, pike-perch and shellfish terrine, steak tartare with salted quail egg) and some intriguing pan-European wines by the glass. (📞09-2709-0976; www.ravintolacarelia.fi; Mannerheimintie 56; 2-/3-course lunch menu €23/29, mains €19-29; ⏰11am-10pm Mon-Thu, 11.30am-11pm Fri, 3-11pm Sat)

Ateljé Finne

FINNISH $$

18 🍴 Map p84, D6

Painted brick walls hung with original art make this bistro an intimate space for refined contemporary Finnish cooking. The short menu has just a handful of choices, but always includes a vegetable, meat and fish dish of the day, bookended by starters such as cold smoked herring croquettes or celeriac salad with roasted yeast, and desserts such as liquorice crème brûlée. (📞010-281-8242; www.ateljefinne.fi; Arkadiankatu 14; mains €23-26, 3-course menu €44; ⏰5-9.30pm Mon-Sat)

KarlJohan

FINNISH $$

19 🍴 Map p84, B7

Welcoming service and an elegant but relaxed atmosphere in a herringbone-floored dining room provide a fitting backdrop for carefully prepared Finnish cuisine, such as *vorschmack* (minced, salty beef and lamb, served with potatoes, pickles and sour cream) and blueberry parfait with mascarpone and rye biscuits. The central location is another plus point. Wines are rather pricey. (📞09-612-1121; www.ravintolakarljohan.fi;

Yrjönkatu 21; mains €18-32; ⏱11am-3pm & 5-11pm Mon-Fri, 2-11pm Sat; 🛜)

Tin Tin Tango
CAFE $

20 Map p84, C4

This buzzy neighbourhood cafe decorated with prints from the quiffed Belgian's adventures has a bit of everything. There's a laundry and a sauna, as well as lunches, brunches and cosy tables where you can sip a drink or get to grips with delicious rolls absolutely stuffed full. The welcoming, low-key bohemian vibe is the real draw, though. (www.tintintango.fi; Töölöntorinkatu 7; dishes €9-12; ⏱7am-midnight Mon-Fri, 9am-midnight Sat, 10am-9pm Sun; 🛜)

Lappi Ravintola
FINNISH $$

21 Map p84, E7

Log-cabin interior cladding, a stone fireplace, hefty timber tables and staff in traditional Sámi dress create an atmospheric backdrop for dining on authentic Lappish specialities such as a game platter for two (€68) with braised reindeer, roast elk, bear sausages, winter vegetables and creamy game sauce. Other dishes include smoked salmon soup and roast snow grouse with cranberry sauce. (☎09-645-550; www.lappires.com; Annankatu 22; mains €23.50-39; ⏱4-10.30pm Mon-Sat)

Salve
FINNISH $$

22 Map p84, C8

Down by the water in the west of town, this 1897-founded establishment has long been a favourite of sailors, and has an appropriately high-seas decor, with paintings of noble ships on the walls. Great Finnish comfort food includes meatballs, fried Baltic herring and steaks in substantial quantities. The atmosphere is warm and the service kindly. (☎010-766-4280; www.raflaamo.fi/fi/helsinki/salve; Hietalahdenranta 5C; mains €18-36; ⏱11am-11pm Mon-Sat, to 10pm Sun)

Konstan Möljä
FINNISH $$

23 Map p84, C8

The maritime interior of this old sailors' eatery, with fishing nets, hooks, brass clocks, lanterns, black-and-white photos and creaking timber floors, is an atmospheric setting for its great-value Finnish buffet for dinner. Though these days it sees plenty of tourists, it serves solid traditional fare (salmon soup, marinated herring, reindeer) with friendly explanations of what goes with what. (☎09-694-7504; www.konstanmolja.fi; Hietalahdenkatu 14; buffet €19; ⏱5-10pm Tue-Fri, 4-11pm Sat)

Naughty Brgr
BURGERS $

24 Map p84, D7

The open kitchen inside this cavernous space sizzles up monumental single-, double- and triple-patty burgers. Alongside meat options such as its signature Naughty Brgr (Finnish beef, blue cheese, bacon jam and aioli) are vegetarian burgers (such as roasted portobello, olive tapenade and lemon-truffle dressing) and a vegan burger (pulled oats, roast tomato, caramelised onion and chipotle cilantro), plus rotating craft beers. (www.naughtybrgr.com; Lönnrotinkatu 13; burgers €10-20; ⏲11am-10pm Tue-Sat, noon-7pm Sun;)

Drinking

Steam Hellsinki COCKTAIL BAR

 25 Map p84, D6

A wonderland of steampunk design, with futuristic-meets-19th-century industrial steam-powered machinery decor, including a giant Zeppelin floating above the gondola-shaped bar, mechanical cogs and pulleys,

globes, lanterns, radios, candelabras, Chesterfield sofas and a Zoltar fortune-telling machine, this extraordinary bar has dozens of varieties of gin and DJs spinning electro-swing. Ask about gin-appreciation and cocktail-making courses in English. (www.steamhellsinki.fi; Olavinkatu 1; ⏲4pm-4am Mon-Sat; 🛜)

A21 COCKTAIL BAR

26 Map p84, E7

At the cutting edge of Helsinki's cocktail scene, this constantly evolving bar revives classic cocktails from past eras, adapts international trends (such as boilermakers, blending craft beers with paired spirits) and crafts new concoctions using Nordic ingredients in cocktails such as Suomen Neito, made with foraged Finnish berries. (www.a21.fi; Annankatu 21; ⏲5pm-midnight Tue & Wed, to 1am Thu, to 2am Fri & Sat)

Vin-Vin WINE BAR

27 Map p84, B8

Glistening mosaic tiles, chandeliers, fringed lamps and vintage velvet sofas make Vin-Vin a super-stylish spot for a glass and a cheese or charcuterie platter, but the natural wines sourced from small vineyards are the main event. Its beer-specialist sibling, Bier-Bier (p73), is in Punavuori. (www.vin-vin.fi; Kalevankatu 6; ⏲4pm-midnight Mon-Fri, 2pm-2am Sat)

 Top Tip

How to Get Tickets

Kamppi and Töölö have some of Helsinki's best entertainment options, from classical concerts held in magnificent churches to jazz clubs, rock venues, cinemas, opera, ballet and spectator sports. Tickets are available online; in the neighbourhood, **Tiketti** (Map p84, D6; www.tiketti.fi; Urho Kekkosenkatu 4; ⏲11am-7pm Mon-Fri) sells tickets to a wide variety of events citywide.

Hietalahden Kauppahalli (p92)

Ateljee Bar

BAR

28 Map p84, B8

An unrivalled panorama of Helsinki unfolds from this tiny 70m-high perch on the 14th floor of the Sokos Hotel Torni. Take the lift to the 12th floor, from where a narrow spiral staircase leads to the top. The bar has a capacity of just 30 people (with 12 more on the glassed-in summer terrace). Minimum age is 20. (www.raflaamo.fi; Sokos Hotel Torni, Yrjönkatu 26; ⏰2pm-1am Mon-Thu, to 2am Fri, noon-2am Sat, 2pm-midnight Sun; 🛜)

Maxine

BAR, CLUB

29 Map p84, D6

On the top of Kamppi shopping centre, this classy venue makes the most of the inspiring city views. It's divided into three sections, with a bar area – a great spot for a sundowner – and two dance floors, one of which (the name, Kirjasto, or Library, gives it away) is quieter. Over 24s only. (www.maxine. fi; 6th fl, Kamppi Shopping Centre, Urho Kekkosenkatu 1A; ⏰10pm-4am Fri & Sat; 🛜)

Bäkkäri

BAR, CLUB

30 Map p84, D6

Central Bäkkäri is devoted to the heavier end of the metal spectrum, with lots of airplay for Finnish legends such as Nightwish, HIM, Children of Bodom and Apocalyptica. It's a classic after-party for bands. Outdoor tables are where the socialising goes on, while upstairs is a club space. Beer's cheap until 8pm. (www.npg.fi/ravintolat/bakkari; Pohjoinen Rautatiekatu 21; ⏱6pm-4am)

U Kaleva   PUB

31 Map p84, B7

Part of a knot of bars on this street just off Mannerheimintie in the heart of town, this unpretentious place stands out for its old-time Finnish atmosphere, cordial owners, eclectic local crowd and heated terrace. (www.ukaleva.fi; Kalevankatu 3A; ⏱2pm-2am)

DTM   GAY, CLUB

32 Map p84, E7

Finland's most famous gay venue (Don't Tell Mama) now occupies smart premises in a very out-of-the-closet location on the city's main street. There are various club nights with variable entry fees. On Saturdays the minimum age for entry is 20. (www.dtm.fi; Mannerheimintie 6B; ⏱9pm-4am; 📶)

Hercules   GAY, CLUB

33 Map p84, C6

Set over three floors, this gay bar is aimed at men aged 30-plus (minimum age on Fridays and Saturdays is 24, and 20 on other days). There's

a lounge bar, basement club and a busy disco with dance-floor classics and campy karaoke. (www.hercules.fi; Pohjoinen Rautatiekatu 21; ⏱9pm-4am)

Entertainment

Finlandia Talo   CONCERT VENUE

34 ⭐ Map p84, D4

Designed by Alvar Aalto, this 1971-completed concert hall in angular white marble is one of Helsinki's landmark buildings. It received its congress wing in 1975 and was expanded in 2011. Alongside a varying program of music, it also mounts art exhibitions. Book tickets through www.lippu.fi. Hour-long guided tours (€15/10 per adult/child) take place in English; check the calendar online. (☎09-40241; www.finlandiatalo.fi; Mannerheimintie 13)

Orion Theatre   CINEMA

35 ⭐ Map p84, D7

Opened in 1927, this gorgeous art deco cinema with chequerboard tiles has 216 plush red seats. It shows classics from the Finnish Film Archive through to new art-house releases, either in English or with English subtitles. (☎029-533-8000; www.kavi.fi; Eerikinkatu 15; tickets adult/child €6.50/3; ⏱screenings Tue-Sun)

Olympic Stadium (p90)

Semifinal
LIVE MUSIC

36 ⭐ Map p84, D7

Next to Tavastia (p83), this smaller sibling has live music almost nightly, with a focus on up-and-coming Finnish bands. Buy tickets on the website or at the door. (☎09-7746-7420; www.tavastiaklubi.fi; Urho Kekkosenkatu 6; ◷8pm-1am Sun-Thu, 9pm-2am Fri, 8pm-4am Sat)

Telia 5G Arena
SPECTATOR SPORT

37 ⭐ Map p84, C1

Next to the Olympic Stadium, this 10,770-seat arena is the home ground of Helsinki's football (aka soccer) team, HJK (Helsingin Jalkapalloklubi). The team is the closest thing Finland has to a Real Madrid or Manchester United, having won 27 league titles at last count. The season runs from April to October. Book tickets online through www.lippu.fi.

The arena's name changes regularly due to corporate sponsorship; in the past it's been known as the Sonera Stadium and the Finnair Stadium. (www.sonerastadium.fi; Urheilukatu 5; tickets €12-15)

Helsingin Jäähalli
SPECTATOR SPORT

38 ⭐ Map p84, C1

Helsinki's second, but more central, venue for ice hockey – after the Hartwall Arena (p127) – is this arena in the Olympic Stadium complex, with

Amos Andersonin Taidemuseo (p88)

a capacity of 8200. (☎09-477-7110; www.helsinginjaahalli.fi; Nordenskiöldinkatu 11-13)

Oopperatalo

OPERA, BALLET

39 ⭐ Map p84, D3

From mid-August to May, opera, ballet and classical concerts are staged at Helsinki's opera house, set in landscaped parkland next to Töölönlahti bay. Designed by Eero Hyvämäki, Jukka Karhunen and Risto Parkkinen, the building was completed in 1993. Performances of the Finnish National

Opera are subtitled in Finnish. Book tickets through www.kippu.fi.

Its main auditorium has a capacity of 1350 seats; the smaller studio seats an audience of 500. (Opera House; ☎09-4030-2211; www.oopperabaletti.fi; Helsinginkatu 58)

Storyville

JAZZ

40 ⭐ Map p84, D5

Helsinki's number-one jazz club attracts a refined older crowd swinging to boogie woogie, trad jazz, Dixieland and New Orleans most nights. As well as the performance space, there's a stylish bar that has a cool outside summer terrace, restaurant and outdoor charcoal grill in the park opposite, where some summer concerts also take place. (☎050-363-2664; www. storyville.fi; Museokatu 8; ☺jazz club 7pm-3am Thu, to 4am Fri & Sat, bar 7pm-2am Tue, to 3am Wed & Thu, to 4am Fri & Sat)

Shopping

Scandinavian Outdoor

SPORTS & OUTDOORS

41 Map p84, A7

If you're heading into the Finnish wilderness, this vast three-level store in the Forum Shopping Centre has your needs covered. On the ground floor there are boots and backpacks, on the 1st floor you'll find clothing, skis, skates and snowshoes; the 2nd floor has tents, sleeping bags, first-aid kits, safety equipment, torches, hiking maps and other accessories.

There's a discount outlet branch near the airport. (www.scandinavianoutdoor.fi; Forum Shopping Centre, Yrjönkatu 29; ☺10am-8pm Mon-Fri, to 6pm Sat, noon-6pm Sun)

Alnilam

ART, ANTIQUES

42 Map p84, D7

Globes in a dizzying array of colours and sizes (some illuminated as lamps), maps, compasses, telescopes, kaleidoscopes, hot-air balloon sculptures, hourglasses, clocks and barometers, both new and antique, are among the exquisite items at this wanderlust-inspiring boutique. (www.alnilam.fi; Lönnrotinkatu 15; ☺10am-5pm Mon-Fri, to 3pm Sat, closed early Jul-early Aug)

Moomin Shop

TOYS, BOOKS

43 Map p84, E6

All things Moomin are sold at this official shop, including author and illustrator Tove Jansson's classic books in English and Finnish. Branches include one at Helsinki's airport. (www.moomin. com; Forum, Mannerheimintie 20; ☺9am-9pm Mon-Fri, to 6pm Sat, noon-6pm Sun)

Levykauppa Äx

MUSIC

44 Map p84, D7

This record shop buys and sells secondhand CDs and vinyl in every imaginable genre. (www.levykauppax. fi; Fredrikinkatu 59; ☺11am-7pm Mon-Fri, to 5pm Sat)

Top Sights
Seurasaaren Ulkomuseo

Getting There

Seurasaaren Ul-komuseo is 5.5km northwest of the city centre. Bus 24 stops outside. Ferries sail to Kuusisaari, 2.2km west. Tram 4 stops 1km north.

Although it's close to the centre, Helsinki's urban tumult feels far away in the most elemental sense at the delightful Seurasaaren Ulkomuseo. Spread over the densely forested island of Seurasaari, the charming 18th- to 20th-century wooden buildings at this open-air museum wing you back to a bygone era, enhanced by guides dressed in traditional costumes who bring the history to life.

Buildings
In all, Seurasaaren Ulkomuseo has 87 historic wooden buildings transferred here from around

Hall in country estate, Seurasaaren Ulkomuseo

Finland. Inside the museum's buildings, guides in traditional costume demonstrate folk dancing and crafts. Replicating the country's geography, the northern section has buildings from Lapland, while the southern section has buildings from Finland's southern regions.

In the northern section, highlights include the **Niemelä tenant farm**, which was the first set of buildings to be relocated here in 1909. Dating from 1844, the farm's buildings incorporate a traditional smoke sauna, cowshed, pig sty and horse stable, a milk storeroom and a boathouse. Also in the northern section, look out for the **Kahiluoto manor house**, built in 1755 and relocated here in 1926. The two-storey building has 13 rooms – downstairs, the dining and drawing rooms have original Gustavian cloth wallpaper, while upstairs, bedrooms are decorated with Biedermeier and neo-rococo furniture.

In the southern section, **Selkämä** is a humble 1786-built smoke-heated farmhouse with attic sleeping quarters, a small kitchen and a granary. Dating from 1730, the more upper-class **Ivars farmstead** has been previously used as an inn, when guests included Tsar Alexander I in 1819.

Other museum buildings include windmills, watermills, churches and stables. Boats on display include tar boats, once used for transporting tar, as well as beautiful giant rowboats used to transport churchgoing communities.

The Grounds

Although the museum itself is only open from mid-May to mid-September, the island is accessible year-round, and you're free to wander the birch and spruce woodland; look out for hares and almost-tame squirrels.

Seurasaari is home to one of Finland's three naturist beaches, with separate sections for men and women.

Seurasaari Open-Air Museum

www.kansallismuseo.fi/en/seurasaari-openairmuseum

Seurasaari

adult/child €9/3

⊙11am-5pm Jun-Aug, 9am-3pm Mon-Fri, 11am-5pm Sat & Sun mid-late May & early–mid-Sep

☑ Top Tips

▶ There are guided tours of the museum in English at 3pm daily from mid-June to mid-August (included in admission).

▶ In May and September, the museum's admission price drops to €6 for adults.

▶ Seurasaari is the venue for Helsinki's biggest midsummer bonfires.

✗ Take a Break

Several museum buildings house atmospheric cafes.

Seurasaari has some picturesque picnic spots, so consider setting up al fresco in fine weather.

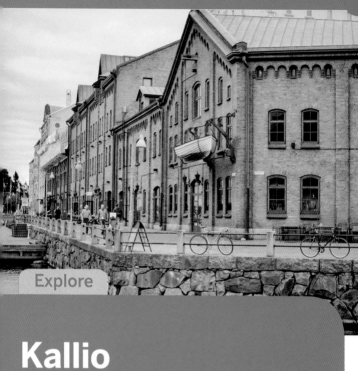

Explore

Kallio

Traditionally a working-class neighbourhood, Kallio is rapidly gentrifying to become one of Helsinki's most up-and-coming areas. Repurposed post-industrial venues here buzz with creative activity – from food labs to a cutting-edge distillery – with public art continuing to pop up throughout its streets, parks and squares.

The Sights in a Day

Start your day in Kallio at **Good Life Coffee** (p110), with some jazzy tunes, sweet treats and locally roasted coffee. If you're travelling with kids, head straight to **Linnanmäki** (p107) amusement park for thrills or **Sea Life** (p107) aquarium for underwater exploration.

Stop for lunch at the traditional market hall, **Hakaniemen Kauppahalli** (p110). Check out the northern harbour, before heading to the trio of streets of Helsinginkatu, Vaasankatu and Hämeentie to discover one-off shops, eateries and bars. The **Kotiharjun Sauna** (p108) is a truly authentic local experience.

Just northeast of here, the former slaughterhouse complex, **Teurastamo** (p105), is a linchpin of Kallio's scene, with some great places to eat and drink, and regular DJs and live gigs.

For a local's day in Kallio, see p104.

 Local Life

Creative Kallio (p104)

 Best of Kallio

Eating
Silvoplee (p110)

Drinking & Nightlife
Helsinki Distillery Company (p105)

Good Life Coffee (p110)

Juttutupa (p111)

Kuudes Linja (p110)

Shopping
Fargo (p105)

Fennica Records (p111)

Getting There

Ⓜ **Metro** Hakaniemi metro station, in the south, is handy for Kallio's waterfront and the Hakaniemen kauppahalli (market hall). To the northeast, Sörnäinen metro station is the most convenient stop for the neighbourhood's bars and offbeat boutiques.

🚊 **Tram** Trams 3, 6, 7 and 9 serve Kallio from the city centre; all pass by Helsinki's train station (p141). Line 8 crosses from Töölö and continues north.

Local Life
Creative Kallio

Kallio is one of Helsinki's hotbeds of creativity, and on this walk through the up-and-coming hood you'll see why. The area teems with public sculptures, cool art-filled cafes, vintage shops stocking homewares and vinyl, and repurposed industrial venues such as a former slaughterhouse that's now home to a distillery.

❶ Reflections

Made from glass plates set between polished aluminium, the 1977 sculpture **Reflections** (Heijastuksia; Sörnäinen) by Helsinki artist Risto Salonen (1945–2001) stands on the Merihaka waterfront and, as its name implies, reflects the surrounding ground, water and sky.

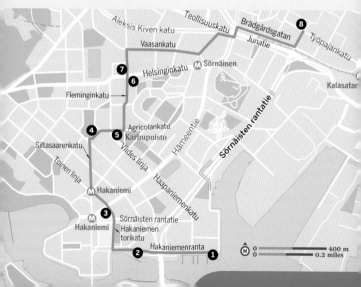

2 Peace Statue

The work of Russian sculptor Oleg Kirjuhin (1929–91), the striking bronze statue **World Peace** (Maailman rauha; Siltasaari) stands 6.5m high and was installed in 1990 as a gift from Moscow. Five life-size figures representing five continents are depicted holding up a foliage-enveloped globe.

3 Modernist Scupture

Made from steel and measuring 3m in diameter, minimalistic, mirror-like **The Symbol** (Symboli; Siltasaarenkatu 18) is a sphere created by Helsinki sculptor Hannu Sirén (b 1953) in 1985 and installed here across from the Hakaniemen kauppahalli.

4 Lutheran Church

Designed by Lars Sonck and completed in 1912, the 65m-high Lutheran church **Kallion Kirkko** (Kallio Church; www.kallionseurakunta.fi; Itäinen Papinkatu 2; admission free; ⏱7am-2pm Mon-Fri, 9am-7pm Sat & Sun) is visible from all over the city. Built from grey granite and topped with a domed copper roof, it is a classic example of National Romantic art nouveau style. Four of the tower's seven bronze bells play a Sibelius composition daily at noon and 6pm.

5 Sculpture in the Park

Carved in red granite in 1931, the **Bear on the Anthill** (Mesikämmen muurahaispesällä) statue in the small park of Karhupuisto (p108) depicts Finland's national symbol, a bear, trying to prise open an anthill. The artist, Jussi Mäntynen (1886–1978), was a taxidermist at Helsinki University's Department of Zoology who was renowned for his lifelike portrayals of animals.

6 Coffee and Art

Virtually everything is vegetarian or vegan at red-brick cafe **Rupla** (www.rupla.fi; Helsinginkatu 16; snacks €2.50-5.50, weekday lunch buffet €9.50, weekend brunch €23; ⏱7.30am-8pm Mon-Fri, 11am-5pm Sat & Sun; 🛜🖊), which has its own Helsinki-roasted coffee blends. Exhibitions by local artists change every three to four weeks. Special events include vintage furniture and clothing sales and DJs.

7 Vintage Shopping

Vintage homewares from the 1950s, '60s and '70s, such as Finnish-designed lamps, chandeliers, crockery, vases, furniture and clocks, are scattered haphazardly throughout **Fargo** (www.fargoshop.fi; Fleminginkatu 20; ⏱3-7pm Tue-Thu, noon-4pm Fri & Sat). Music fans will love the racks of vinyl from the same era, as well as retro music and movie posters.

8 Food and Beer

Former abattoir area **Teurastamo** (https://teurastamo.com; Työpajankatu 2; ⏱9am-9pm Mon & Tue, to 10pm Wed-Sat, to 8pm Sun) has eateries offering dim sum, smokehouse (p110) fare, pasta, artisan ice-cream and more. Also here is the Helsinki Distillery Company (p108), which runs tours and has a raw-concrete in-house bar.

For reviews see

◎ Sights	p107
⊗ Eating	p108
⊗⊗⊗ Drinking	p110
⊗ Entertainment	p111
⊕ Shopping	p111

0 — 400 m
0 — 0.2 miles

Gulf of Finland

Helsinki Distillery Company

Vähä laivlue

Kalasatama

Työpajankatu

Sörnäistenkatu

Brädgärdsgatan

Pääskylänkatu

Junatie

Hämeentie

Mäkelänkatu

Hämeentie

Sörnäisten rantatie

Teollisuuskatu

Aleksis Kiven katu

Vaasankatu

Sörnäinen

Harjutorinkatu

Kaikukuja

Lintulahdenkatu

Hämeentie

Kaikukatu

Näkinsilta

Hakaniemenkatu

Pohjoisranta

Fleminginkatu

Helsinginkatu

Kaarlenkatu

Agricolankatu

Karhupuisto

Porthaninkatu

Hakaniemi

Sörnäisten Rantatie

Hakaniementori (Hakaniemi Market Square)

Castréninkatu

KALLIO

Siltasaarenkatu

Suoniokatu

Hakaniemi

HAKANIEMI

Hakaniemi

Siltasaarenkatu

Säästöpankinranta

Pitkänsillanranta

Kirstinkatu

Suvrenkatu

Kolmas linja

Töinen linja

Ensi linja

Eläintarhantie

Työväenmuseo

Linnanmäki

Sea Life

Helsinginkatu

Aleksis Kiven katu

Töölönlahti

Kaisaniemenpuisto

University Botanical Gardens

◎9 ⊗4 ◎3 ◎16 ⊗13 ⊗14 ⊗12 ⊗6 ⊗8 ⊗11 ⊗10 ⊗15 ⊗7 ◎5 ◎1 ◎2

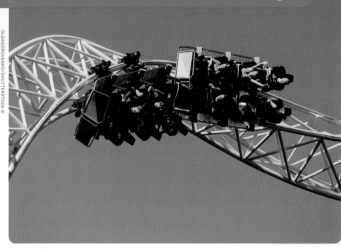

Linnanmäki

Sights

Linnanmäki   AMUSEMENT PARK

1 ⊙ Map p106, A2

Famous Linnanmäki is a real kid pleaser with rides (some free) including several roller coasters and a panoramic 75m free-fall tower, as well as nightly fireworks. Its profits are donated to child-welfare organisations. There are various day passes, some of which discount admission to nearby Sea Life. Cheaper tickets available online. It's closed from November to late April, and hours vary greatly outside mid-June to August, so check the website's calendar. Bus 23 and trams 3 and 8 take you here. (www.

linnanmaki.fi; Tivolikuja 1; single ride/day pass €8/39, combination ticket with Sea Life €47; ⊙11am-10pm mid-Jun–Aug, hours vary late Apr–mid-Jun, Sep & Oct)

Sea Life   AQUARIUM

2 ⊙ Map p106, A2

Close to Linnanmäki, Sea Life is an enjoyable aquarium complex with walk-through tunnels that let you spot sharks, rays, octopuses and myriad fish up close. Space is limited, so booking ahead online is advised. Online bookings also offer a small discount. Take bus 23 or trams 3 or 9. (☏09-565-8200; www.visitsealife.com; Tivolitie 10; adult/child €16.50/13, combination

OLGAGOROVENKO/SHUTTERSTOCK ©

ticket with Linnanmäki €47; ⊘10am-8pm Jun–mid-Aug, hours vary mid-Aug–May)

Työväenasuntomuseo   MUSEUM

3 Map p106, B1

In a charming wooden house built in 1909, this delightful museum shows how industrial workers lived in the early 20th century, with nine rooms decorated according to different eras. Its on-site shop stocks homewares that are not only inspired by times gone by but are practical today, too.

Stairs mean it's not accessible for visitors with disabilities. (Museum of Worker Housing; www.tyovaenasuntomuseo.

fi; Kirstinkuja 4; admission free; ⊘11am-5pm Wed-Sun early May–mid-Oct)

Helsinki Distillery Company   DISTILLERY

4 Map p106, D1

At the former slaughterhouse Teurastamo (p105), the Helsinki Distillery Company produces unique spirits using Finnish ingredients, including single-malt and rye whiskies, gin, akvavit, apple jack, sea buckthorn brandy and lingonberry liqueur. Tours lasting 25 minutes take you behind the scenes. Upstairs, its raw concrete bar is a great place to sample its wares and hosts occasional live music. (☎020-719-1460; www.hdco.fi; Työpajankatu 2A, Teurastamo; tours €15; ⊘tours in English 5pm Wed, bar 5pm-midnight Wed & Thu, to 2am Fri & Sat)

Karhupuisto   PARK

5 Map p106, C2

In the heart of Kallio, this small park is lined by maple trees and has beautiful floral displays in spring and summer. Look out for the *Bear on the Anthill* (p104), sculpted by taxidermist Jussi Mäntynen in 1931. (Fleminginkatu)

Local Life

Kotiharjun Sauna

Helsinki's only original traditional public wood-fired sauna, **Kotiharjun Sauna** (Map p106, C2; www.kotiharjunsauna.fi; Harjutorinkatu 1; adult/child €13/7; ⊘2-9.30pm Tue-Sun) dates back to 1928. It's a classic experience, where you can also get a scrub down and massage (from €30). There are separate saunas for men and women; bring your own towel or rent one (€3). It's a 150m stroll southwest of the Sörnäinen metro station.

This type of place largely disappeared with the advent of shared saunas in apartment buildings, although a recent resurgence has seen several new public saunas being opened in the city.

Eating

Kuja   BISTRO $

6 Map p106, C4

An upbeat young team helms this hip little bistro across from the water-

GRISHA BRUEV/SHUTTERSTOCK ©

Sea Life (p107)

front. Burgers are a highlight, with choices including pulled pork (with noodles and chilli sauce), salmon (with pickled cucumber and slaw) and tofu (with roasted bell peppers), with the option of gluten-free buns. There are gourmet salads, savoury crêpes, *flammkuchen* (thin-crusted Alsatian pizza) and over 30 craft beers.

Vegetarian options (including vegan choices) abound. (☏040-046-1008; www.kujabarbistro.fi; Hakaniemenkatu 7; mains €13-23; ⊙10.30am-10pm Mon & Tue, to 11pm Wed & Thu, to midnight Fri, 11.30am-midnight Sat, 11.30am-9pm Sun; 🛜🖉)

Flying Dutch GASTROPUB $

7 ✖ Map p106, B4

Built in 1897 in the Netherlands, this timber boat makes a great stop for a craft beer or cider up on deck or dockside tables, but it's an even better bet for food, from salmon soup and *skagen* (prawn-topped toast) to burgers such as pulled duck with truffle-champagne sauce, or goat's cheese with caramelised sweet potato, avocado and harissa mayo. (www.pikkudami. com; Pitkänsillanranta 2; mains €15-16.50; ⊙kitchen noon-8pm Mon-Sat, to 7pm Sun, bar to midnight Mon-Sat, to 10pm Sun)

Hakaniemen Kauppahalli

MARKET $

8 Map p106, B3

This traditional-style Finnish food market hall sits right by the Hakaniemi metro station. With over 50 stalls, there's a great range of produce and a cafe, with textile outlets upstairs. An outdoor market sets up on the square in summer. (www.hakaniemenkauppahalli. fi; Hämeentie 1; ◷8am-6pm Mon-Fri, to 4pm Sat; 🖉)

B-Smokery

BARBECUE $

9 Map p106, E1

B-Smokery pays homage to the Teurastamo (p105) former slaughterhouse with meats smoked in its Texan smoker using apple wood, and cooked in its stainless-steel open kitchen amid exposed brick and concrete post-industrial surrounds. Babyback ribs with Helsinki Distillery Company (p105) whisky glaze, pastrami or bris-

---

Top Tip

Safe Travel

While gentrification continues apace here, parts of the area still retain a gritty character and can have an edgier feel than some of Helsinki's more affluent neighbourhoods. As in any big city, keep your wits about you and avoid walking alone in unlit areas after dark. This character, however, gives rise to some fantastic creative spaces and a brilliant bar scene.

---

ket sandwiches and chicken wings are among its specialities. There's always one veggie dish of the day. (📞040-777-5959; www.bsmokery.fi; Työpajankatu 2C, Teurastamo; mains €14-21; ◷11am-10pm Tue-Fri, 1-10pm Sat; 🖥)

Silvoplee

VEGETARIAN $

10 Map p106, B3

At this large, light-filled cafe with blond wood counters, brightly painted pillars and tiled floors, vegetarian food (including vegan options) is sold by weight. Around 80% of ingredients are locally sourced, and around 60% are organic. (www.silvoplee.fi; Toinen linja 7; soup/mains per 1kg €17.80/22.30; ◷8am-7pm Mon-Fri, 9am-6pm Sat; 🖥🖉)

Drinking

Good Life Coffee

CAFE

11 🍷 Map p106, B3

Lime-green light fittings, geometric wallpaper, framed photography and art, and turntables spinning jazz make Good Life a great neighbourhood hang-out. Aeropress coffee prepared from locally roasted beans is served alongside homemade cakes, pastries and cookies. (www.goodlifecoffee.fi; Kolmas Linja 17; ◷8am-6pm Mon-Fri, 9am-4pm Sat; 🖥)

Kuudes Linja

CLUB

12 🍷 Map p106, C3

Between Hakaniemi and Sörnäinen metro stations, this famed club is the place to find Helsinki's more experimental beats from top visiting DJs playing techno, industrial, post-rock and electro. There are also live gigs (invariably metal). Entry is free on Thursday and generally starts from €12 on other nights. (www.kuudeslinja.com; Hämeentie 13B; ⊙10pm-4am Wed, Fri & Sat, 11pm-4am Thu)

Fairytale
GAY & LESBIAN

 13 Map p106, C2

One of Kallio's darkened drinking dens, this small, unassuming bar is frequented by both men and women. The front terrace is a prime streetside spot. (www.fairytale.fi; Helsinginkatu 7; ⊙4pm-2am Mon-Fri, 2pm-2am Sat & Sun; 🛜)

Roskapankki
PUB

 14 Map p106, B2

A Kallio classic, this dive bar has some of Helsinki's cheapest beer, a soundtrack of metal and rock, and great ragged character. The action spills onto the pavement terrace in warm weather. (Helsinginkatu 20; ⊙9am-2am)

Entertainment

Juttutupa
LIVE MUSIC

15 Map p106, B4

A block from Hakaniemi metro station, in an enormous granite build-

ing, Juttutupa is one of Helsinki's better bars for live music, focusing on contemporary jazz and rock fusion. All gigs are free. There's a great beer terrace and an on-site sauna. (☎020-742-4240; www.juttutupa.fi; Säästöpankin-ranta 6; ⊙bar 10.30am-midnight Mon & Tue, to 1am Wed & Thu, to 3am Fri, 11am-3am Sat, noon-11pm Sun)

Shopping

Fennica Records
MUSIC

 16 Map p106, D2

Fennica stocks new and secondhand CDs and vinyl from Suomi pop to soul and jazz. (☎09-685-1433; www.fennicakeskus.fi; Hämeentie 21; ⊙10am-6pm Mon-Fri, to 3pm Sat)

Local Life
Porvoo

Finland's second-oldest town, Porvoo (Swedish: Borgå) was officially founded in 1380. The historic Vanha Porvoo is famous for its oft-photographed riverside warehouses and the colourful wooden houses that line the cobblestone streets. The Old Town is also peppered with enough cafes and confectioners to satisfy any sweet tooth.

Getting There

🚍 From Kamppi, buses run to Porvoo every 30 minutes (€9 to €15, one hour).

⛴ In summer, the noble steamship *JL Runeberg* (one way/return €27/39) cruises from the kauppatori to Porvoo.

❶ Landmark Cathedral

Porvoo's magnificent stone-and-timber **Tuomiokirkko** (www.porvoonseurakunnat. fi; ⏱10am-2pm Tue-Sat, 2-4pm Sun Oct-Apr, 10am-6pm Mon-Fri, to 2pm Sat, 2-5pm Sun May-Sep) sits atop a hill overlooking the quaint Old Town. This is where Tsar Alexander I convened the first Diet of Finland in 1809, giving Finland religious freedom.

❷ Old-Fashioned Eats

This rambling 18th-century log building houses the renowned **Wanha Laamanni** (☎020-752-8355; www.wanha laamanni.fi; Vuorikatu 17; mains €20-30, tasting menu €60; ⏱11am-11pm Mon-Sat, noon-8pm Sun) The restaurant offers a classy menu of Finnish favourites and a six-course surprise menu. The setting is inviting, with a roaring fireplace inside and a sprawling terrace with views to the river.

❸ Old Town Square

At the heart of the Old Town, Porvoo's charming cobbled square is home to a summer market and the local **museum** (www.porvoonmuseo.fi; Jokikatu 45; adult/child €8/free; ⏱10am-4pm Mon-Sun May-Aug, noon-4pm Wed-Sun Sep-Apr), housed in the town hall (Vanha Raatihuoneentori).

❹ Dessert Cafe

Tantalise your sweet tooth at the delightful **Cafe Postres** (www.cafepostres.fi; Gabriel Hagertinkuja; ⏱10am-6pm Mon-Fri, to 4pm Sat), brainchild of Michelin-starred chef Samuli Wirgentius. Take your pick from rich, creamy gelato and to-die-for desserts, or sample the savoury open-face smørrebrød sandwiches on house-made sourdough bread.

❺ Runeberg Tortes

A kindly Russian grandmother would happily sip tea in the courtyard of the **Helmi Tea & Coffee House** (www. porvoonhelmet.net; Välikatu 7; cakes €3-7; ⏱11am-6pm Mon-Sat, to 4pm Sun). It's famous for its Runeberg torte (almond-rum cake, topped with raspberry jam).

❻ Sweet Treats

The Brunberg family has been making legendary chocolate and liquorice delights in Porvoo for more than a century. Sample them at the **Brunberg sweet shop** (www.brunberg.fi; Välikatu 4; ⏱10am-6pm Mon-Fri, 9am-4pm Sat, 10am-4pm Sun).

❼ Down by the Riverside

Next to the main bridge, **Porvoon Paahtimo** (www.porvoonpaahtimo.fi; Mannerheiminkatu 2; ⏱10am-midnight Sun-Thu, to 3am Fri & Sat) is an atmospheric red-brick former storehouse that is an ideal spot for drinks, whether house-roasted coffee or beers on tap. There's a riverside terrace, with blankets on offer for cooler evenings. And nothing represents Porvoo better than the picturesque **rust-red storehouses** that line the Porvoonjoki. Some now house delightful guesthouses or summer cafes. Snap the best photo from the bridge.

Top Sights
Tuusulanjärvi

Getting There

Mäntsälä-bound buses from Kamppi bus station travel here on weekdays. You could also make a bike tour of it, taking the train to Kerava and back from Järvenpää.

The views from the narrow stretch of road running along Tuusulanjärvi (Tuusula Lake), 35km north of Helsinki, inspired some of Finland's greatest artists. Museums here include composer Sibelius' home, Ainola; painter Pekka Halonen's studio and home, Halosenniemi; and the Lottamuseo, commemorating the Lotta women's voluntary defence force.

Ainola

Finland's finest composer Jean Sibelius was among the heroes of the National Romantic movement to call the lake region of Tuusulanjärvi home. Sibelius'

Ainola

family **home** (www.ainola.fi; Ainolankatu, Järvenpää; adult/child €8/2; ⊙10am-5pm Tue-Sun May-Sep), designed by Lars Sonck and built on this forested site in 1904, contains original furniture, paintings, books and a piano on which Sibelius plotted out tunes until his death. The graves of Jean Sibelius and his wife Aino are in the property's garden.

Halosenniemi

One of the most notable museums in the lakeside region of Tuusulanjärvi is **Halosenniemi** (www.halosenniemi.fi; Halosenniementie 4-6, Järvenpää; adult/child €8/2; ⊙11am-6pm Tue-Sun May-Aug, noon-5pm Tue-Sun Sep-Apr). The sizeable Karelian-inspired log-built studio and home of Pekka Halonen (1865–1933) has changing exhibitions of works by Halonen himself and his contemporaries. It's a lovely place with great views and a lakeside garden.

Lottamuseo

This striking blue Tuusulanjärvi **building** (www.lottamuseo.com; Rantatie 39, Järvenpää; adult/child €6/1; ⊙9am-6pm Tue-Sun May-Sep, 10am-5pm Tue-Sun Oct-Apr) commemorates the Lotta women's voluntary defence force, established in 1921 after the independence of Finland. Named for a character in a JL Runeberg poem, these unarmed women took on military service during WWII to become one of the world's largest auxiliaries. Look out among the military paraphernalia for the blue-and-white crux gammata and heraldic silver rose medals, which many Lottas wore.

☑ **Top Tips**

▶ Thirty-minute guided tours at Ainola and Lottamuseo are included in the entrance fees, but they must be booked in advance.

▶ At Ainola, garden tours are also available on Thursdays - at noon in English (July only) and at 2pm and 4pm in Finnish.

▶ Learn more about this region at **Visit Lake Tuusula** (www.visittuusulanjarvi.fi).

☑ **Take a Break**

Have lunch at Ainola's Cafe Aulis, where big picture windows overlook the lush gardens.

The cosy Canteen at the Lottamuseo serves soup, salad and a daily-changing lunch special (€6 to €9), as well as traditional pastries and ever-uplifting coffee.

The Best of
Helsinki

Helsinki's Best Walks

Architectural Stroll.............. 118

Green Helsinki.................. 120

Helsinki's Best...

Eating 122

Drinking & Nightlife............. 124

Entertainment 126

Shopping........................ 128

History 130

Art & Architecture................ 132

Outdoors 134

Saunas 135

For Kids........................ 136

For Free........................ 137

Tours........................... 138

Temppeliaukion Kirkko (p89), designed by architects Timo and Tuomo Suomalainen
KIEV.VICTOR/SHUTTERSTOCK ©

Best Walks
Architectural Stroll

🏃 The Walk

Helsinki is renowned for its architecture, and this walk takes in many exemplars of the city's dramatically varying styles, while also peeling away the layers of the city's history. Along this photogenic route you'll see its evolution from market town to the cutting-edge Nordic capital that is Helsinki today.

Start Vanha Kauppahalli

Finish Temppeliaukion Kirkko

Length 3.2km; three hours

✗ Take a Break

Vanha Kauppahalli (p65)

Karl Fazer Café (p33)

GRISHA BRIEV/SHUTTERSTOCK ©

Uspenskin Katedraali (p45)

❶ Havis Amanda

The symbol of Helsinki is the bronze **Havis Amanda** (p43), the female nude statue dipping in a fountain, which was installed in 1908.

❷ Kauppatori

The bustling **kauppatori** (market square; p48) is flanked by stately 19th-century buildings, including the **Presidentinlinna** (Presidential Palace; p43), which was designed by architect CL Engel. The eagle-topped stone obelisk is the 1835 Keisarinnankivi (Empress' Stone), Helsinki's oldest monument, honouring a visit by Tsar Nicholas I and Tsarina Alexandra.

❸ Orthodox Cathedral

Strolling east you can't miss the gleaming gold onion domes of the **Uspenskin Katedraali** (p45). Built as a Russian Orthodox church in 1868, it now serves the Finnish Orthodox congregation. Look for the turreted National Romantic art nouveau villas nearby.

❹ Lutheran Cathedral

Head up Sofiankatu to Senaatintori (p45). Engel's stately neoclassical **Tuomiokirkko** (p45) is topped by zinc statues of the 12 apostles on the roof.

❺ Ateneum

Walk west to the country's finest art museum, the **Ateneum** (p24), in a palatial 1887 neo-Renaissance building designed by Finnish architect Theodor Höijer.

❻ Train Station

National Romantic splendour reaches its peak at Helsinki's spectacular **train station** (p141), topped by a copper-caped clock tower, which opened in 1919.

❼ Kiasma

A dramatic contrast awaits just west at the **Kiasma museum** (p26), the curved metallic lines of which were unveiled in 1998.

❽ Parliament House

Continue walking northwest. Monolithic **Parliament House** (p89) dominates this stretch. Opposite you'll see the striking glass-and-copper Musiikkitalo (p35), with concert halls and studios.

❾ Stone Church

Venture west through leafy backstreets to the **Temppeliaukion Kirkko** (p89), an extraordinary church hewn from solid rock in 1969.

Best Walks
Green Helsinki

🏃 The Walk

Flower-filled parks and rambling gardens cover one third of Helsinki's total area, making it a wonderfully green escape – during the summer months, at least. Choose a warm, sunny day for this city-wide stroll when you can see the 'outdoor living rooms' of the capital's inhabitants at their leafiest and most lively.

Start Kajsaniemi

Finish Löyly Sauna

Length 5km; four hours

🍴 Take a Break

Vanha Kauppahalli (p65)

Anton & Anton (p47)

Facade detail, Helsinki train station (p31)

MAYLAT/SHUTTERSTOCK ©

❶ Kajsaniemi

The city's central botanic gardens, **Kajsaniemi** (p28), make an ideal starting point for this stroll. Allow time to wander its 10 interconnected greenhouses sheltering 800 plant species from environments around the globe.

❷ Rautatientori

Make your way south to **Rautatientori** (p31), dominated by Helsinki's glorious art nouveau train station. There's almost always live entertainment, such as buskers, in the large open space; a vast ice rink sets up here in winter.

❸ Esplanadin Puisto

Continuing south brings you to **Esplanadin Puisto** (p31), an elegant strip of green in the heart of the city's business district. It's flanked on both sides by some of Helsinki's most upmarket designer boutiques.

4 Observatory Hill Park

From the eastern end of Esplanadin Puisto, it's a short stroll south to **Observatory Hill Park** (p62), with winding woodland paths and blooming tulips and other bulbs. The park is named for its 1834-built observatory, which is now an astronomical museum.

5 Kaivopuisto

Walking further south along tree-lined streets takes you to the seaside park of **Kaivopuisto** (p64), with superb views of fortress Suomenlinna and the Helsinki archipelago's islands. There's a beach, bars and cafes, and there's an observatory here too, dating from 1926, which occasionally opens to the public.

6 Löyly Sauna

Head west along the waterfront, passing boats bobbing in the marinas, to the striking timber structure housing **Löyly Sauna** (p65). Opened in 2016, the wind- and water-powered complex has three saunas, including a traditional smoke sauna, and direct access to the water out front for a dip between steam sessions. Finish with a beer at its panoramic glassed-in bar.

Best
Eating

Finnish cuisine has been influenced by both Sweden and Russia and draws on the local bounty: fish, game, meat, milk and potatoes, with dark rye used to make bread and porridge, and few spices employed. Helsinki's restaurants feature Finnish classics, modern Suomi cuisine and international dishes. Don't miss the produce-laden outdoor markets in summer and wonderful market halls year-round.

Staples

Soup A Finnish favourite. Heavy pea, meat or cabbage soups are traditional workers' fare, while creamier fish soups have a more delicate flavour.

Fish A mainstay of the Finnish diet, including fresh or smoked *lohi* (salmon), *silli* (marinated herring), *lavaret* (siika, a lake whitefish), *kuha* (pike-perch or zander) and delicious *nieriä* or *rautu* (Arctic char).

Meat Reindeer has always been a staple food for the Sámi in the northern latitudes. The traditional way to eat it is sautéed with lingonberries. Elk is also eaten, mostly in hunting season.

New Nordic Cuisine

Riding the wave of new Nordic cuisine is a breed of Finnish chef experimenting with traditional ingredients such as lake fish, berries, wild mushrooms, reindeer and other seasonal produce in decidedly untraditional fashion. A slew of gourmet contemporary Finnish restaurants in Helsinki offer exquisite multicourse tasting menus that make a great contrast to the heavier, sauce-laden typical cuisine.

☑ Top Tips

▶ Service is included in bills, so tipping is not necessary, but it's common to leave a few extra euros for exceptional service.

▶ Reservations aren't usually required at lunch, except at popular and/or top-end addresses. Busy weekend brunch spots should be booked ahead where possible.

▶ In the evening, reserving ahead is generally a good idea as popular places can book out fast.

Best Eating

Grön Foraged ingredients by the artists who create its ceramic plates and paintings. (p83)

Olo Widely considered Helsinki's premier destination restaurant. (p46)

Vanha Kauppahalli Helsinki's 19th-century central market hall is a civic treasure. (p65)

Savoy One of Helsinki's grandest dining rooms, designed by Alvar and Aino Aalto. (p66)

Saaristo Island setting and famous crayfish parties. (p109)

Best Traditional Finnish

Konstan Möljä Old sailor's restaurant filled with maritime paraphernalia. (p93)

Kosmos Classics served in 1924 Aalto-designed premises. (p91)

Kolme Kruunua Frill-free Finnish favourites in a retro '50s dining room. (p47)

Saaga Rustic Lappish decor and superb dishes from the north. (p67)

Best Contemporary Finnish

Grön Exquisitely presented, exceptional-value dishes. (p83)

Demo One of Helsinki's hottest addresses for contemporary Finnish fare. (p66)

Kuu Contemporary twists on Finnish ingredients. (p91)

Ateljé Finne Short but stellar menu of contemporary Finnish fare. (p92)

Best Vegetarian

Story Vegetarian options abound at this cafe inside the Vanha Kauppahalli market hall. (p66)

Zucchini All-vegetarian restaurant that offers a good range of vegan dishes. (p69)

Silvoplee Veggie and vegan food at this Kallio cafe is sold by weight. (p110)

Best for Families

Mumin Kaffe Adorable cafe featuring Moomin prints, crockery, glassware and books for sale. (p47)

Karl Fazer Café Adults and kids alike love the grand setting, great food and dazzling displays of chocolates. (p33)

Goodwin A cow statue lounges outside this steak restaurant, which has inexpensive kids menus. (p70)

Skiffer Excellent pizzas here also come in smaller sizes for kids. (p69)

Island Dining

Most renowned of Helsinki's island restaurants is the **Saaristo** (🕾09-7425-5590; www.ravintolasaaristo.fi; Luoto; mains €21-42, crayfish parties per person €67; ⏰by reservation 5-11pm Mon-Fri May-Sep), set in a spire-crowned art nouveau villa on Luoto (Swedish: Klippan), and famous for society weddings, refined Finnish cuisine and summer crayfish parties. It's reached by private boat from the pier south of the Olympia Terminaali ferry terminal.

Best
Drinking & Nightlife

Diverse drinking and nightlife in Helsinki ranges from cosy bars to specialist craft-beer and cocktail venues, and clubs with live music and DJs. In summer early opening beer terraces sprout all over town. Some club nights have a minimum age of 20 or older; check event details on websites before you arrive.

Coffee

The Finns lead the world in *kahvi* (coffee) consumption, downing more than 20 million cups per day – that's around four per day per person. Cafes are ubiquitous, ranging from 100-year-old imperial classics to local roasteries and drip-filter specialists.

Alcoholic Beverages

Finns drink plenty of *olut* (beer). Among the major local brews are Karhu, Koff, Olvi and Lapin Kulta. The big brands are all lagers, but several craft breweries and microbreweries make excellent light and dark beers. Cider is also popular, as is *lonkero*, a ready-made mix of gin and fruity soft drink, usually grapefruit. Finns don't tend to drink in rounds; everybody pays their own.

Other uniquely Finnish drinks include *salmiakkikossu,* which combines dissolved liquorice sweets with the iconic Koskenkorva vodka (an acquired taste); *fisu,* which does the same but with Fisherman's Friend pastilles; *sahti,* a sweet, high-alcohol beer; and cloudberry or cranberry liqueurs.

☑ Top Tips

▶ On Wednesday nights restaurants are busy, music is playing at all the nightspots, and bars are full – Finns are celebrating *pikku lauantai, or* 'little Saturday'.

Best Drinking & Nightlife

Helsinki Distillery Company Cutting-edge Kallio distillery with a fantastic in-house bar. (p108)

Kaivohuone Unmissable summer club nights in an 1838 beachside pavilion. (p72)

Birri Helsinki's best microbrewery. (p72)

Steam Hellsinki Steampunk-styled bar

mixing serious cocktails. (p94)

Kappeli Grand 19th-century cafe with a terrace overlooking Esplanadin Puisto's bandstand. (p34)

Best Coffee

Kaffa Roastery Warehouse-set roastery with in-house coffee bar. (p71)

La Torrefazione Creates its own roasting profiles. (p34)

Good Life Coffee Kallio coffee specialist. (p110)

Johan & Nyström Set in a fabulous waterfront warehouse. (p41)

Best Craft Beer

Birri Beers brewed on premises in the heart of the Design District. (p72)

Teerenpeli Brews include berry ciders. (p82)

Bier-Bier Connoisseurs' favourite. (p73)

Best Cocktail Bars

A21 Breaking new ground in Helsinki's cocktail scene. (p94)

Steam Hellsinki Gin-appreciation and cocktail-making courses. (p94)

Liberty or Death Speakeasy-style bar mixing rare spirits. (p73)

Best Music Bars

Juttutupa Free live music, beer terrace and sauna. (p111)

Bar Loose Classy rock bar. (p83)

Bäkkäri The heaviest of Helsinki's metal. (p95)

Island Brewery

By the main quay, **Suomenlinnan Panimo** ([☎]020-742-5307; www.panimor avintola.fi; Suomenlinna C1; mains €15-29.50; [⊙]noon-10pm Mon-Sat, to 6pm Sun Jun-Aug, shorter hours Sep-May) is the best place to drink or dine on Suomenlinna. It brews three ciders and seven different beers, including a hefty porter, plus several seasonal varieties, and offers good food to accompany it.

Kuudes Linja Top DJs, experimental beats. (p110)

TheRiff The best Helsinki gigs. (p73)

Best
Entertainment

The arts have long played a major role in Finland's national identity, and as such arts education is a high priority. The result is a flourishing arts scene, especially in Helsinki. A performance of live music is sure to be a highlight of any visit to the capital.

Music

Finland's music scene is one of the world's richest and the output of quality musicians per capita is amazingly high, whether a polished symphony orchestra violinist or a headbanging bassist for the next big death-metal band. Summer in Helsinki and across the country is all about music festivals of every conceivable type.

Theatre

Most theatre productions are in Finnish. The Finnish National Theatre, Kansallisteatteri (p36), is based in a beautiful National Romantic art nouveau building.

Sport

Between September and April, ice hockey reigns supreme; going to a game is a fantastic Helsinki experience. The world championships in May are avidly watched on big screens.

The football (soccer) season runs from April to October; Helsinki's successful local team HJK (Helsingin Jalkapalloklubi) has a passionate following.

☑ Top Tips

▶ The latest events are publicised in the free *Helsinki This Week* (www.helsinki thisweek.com).

▶ Tickets for big events can be purchased from Ticketmaster (www. ticketmaster.fi), Lippupiste (www.lippu. fi) or LiveNation (www.livenation.fi).

▶ Tiketti (www. tiketti.fi) also has a booking office in Kamppi.

Best Classical Music

Musiikkitalo Home to the Helsinki Philharmonic Orchestra, Finnish Radio Symphony

Musiikkitalo (p35)

Orchestra and Sibelius Academy. (p35)

Finlandia Talo Splendid concert hall designed by Alvar Aalto. (p96)

Oopperatalo Helsinki's opera house has a stunning waterfront setting. (p98)

Best Rock & Contemporary Music

Tavastia Legendary venue hosting local and international acts. (p83)

Semifinal A platform for emerging Finnish artists. (p97)

Nosturi Fabulous harbourside warehouse hosting a wide spectrum of gigs. (p75)

Best Jazz

Storyville Helsinki's premier jazz club. (p98)

Musiikkitalo Jazz is frequently on the program at the Helsinki Music Centre. (p35)

Juttutupa Jazz and fusion gigs at this Kallio music bar are free. (p111)

Best Spectator Sport

Helsingin Jäähalli Small but central venue for ice hockey. (p97)

Telia 5G Arena Home ground of Helsinki's football team, HJK (Helsingin Jalkapalloklubi). (p97)

Hartwall Hockey

The best place to see top-level hockey matches is at **Hartwall Arena** (☏ 020-41997; www.hartwall-arena.fi; Areenakuja 1, Pasila), 4km north of the city centre. It's the home of Helsinki's Jokerit ('Jesters') team, which plays in the international Kontinental Hockey League (KHL). Bus 69 from Kamppi bus station stops closest to the stadium at Vaihdemiehenkatu. Alternatively, it's a 1km walk east of Ilmala train station.

Best
Shopping

Helsinki is a design epicentre, from fashion to furniture and homewares. Its hub is the Design District Helsinki (www.designdistrict.fi), spread out between chic Esplanadi to the east, retro-hipster Punavuori to the south and Kamppi to the west. Hundreds of shops, studios and galleries are mapped on the website.

Glassware & Ceramics

The story of the Iittala glass company could be a metaphor for the story of Finnish design. Still copying Swedish models in the early 20th century, the company began to pursue homegrown ideas. From one design competition came Alvar Aalto's famous Iittala vase, which he described as 'an Eskimo woman's leather trousers'. Later, designers explored textures and forms gleaned from Finnish lakescapes, as well as an opaque look which resembled ceramics. Iittala is today under the same ownership as Hackman (cutlery and cookware) and Arabia (ceramics).

Clothing & Jewellery

Though innovative ideas are constantly created, they are built on solid, traditional foundations. For example, the godfather of Finnish design, Kaj Franck borrowed designs from traditional rustic clothing for his pared-back creations. Marimekko, founded in 1951, was the first name in Finnish fashion to make an international impact with its bold optimistic prints.

Other well-established Finnish names include Aarikka, whose wooden jewellery and other accessories have a reassuring solidity and honesty, and Kalevala Koru, a byword for quality silver and gold jewellery.

Best Shopping

Artek Helsinki's city-centre branch of this iconic Aalto-founded company sells unique pieces not found elsewhere. (p36)

Lasikammari Rare vintage Finnish glassware. (p49)

Stockmann Helsinki's largest department store occupies a landmark building. (p37)

Best for Design

Tre City-centre design emporium with cutting-edge creations. (p36)

Jukka Rintala Fashion, wallpapers and more from this renowned designer. (p59)

Aarikka Finnish designs include exquisite jewellery. (p37)

Karl Fazer Café (p33)

Awake Sustainable designs are showcased in this minimalist Design District space. (p59)

Lokal Hybrid gallery-boutique with rotating displays. (p59)

Best for Sweets

Sweet Story Distinctive Finnish sweets made locally in Helsinki. (p49)

Roobertin Herkku Salty liquorices and tar drops are among the specialities of this sweet shop. (p75)

Fazer Famous Fazer chocolates are tantalisingly displayed at its cupola-topped cafe. (p33)

Brunberg Maker of legendary chocolates and liquorice delights in Porvoo. (p113)

Best for Music

Fargo Vintage vinyl (and homewares, too). (p105)

Fennica Records Suomi pop to soul and jazz. (p111)

Levykauppa Äx Stocks a dizzying range of music genres. (p99)

Best for Books

Akateeminen Kirjakauppa An Alvar Aalto–designed building houses Finland's biggest bookshop. (p37)

Nide Art, architecture and design books are a speciality. (p59)

Design Museum The bookshop inside Helsinki's Design Museum has a superb range of titles. (p56)

Arabia Centre

Arabiakeskus (www.arabia.fi; Hämeentie 135, Toukola; noon–6pm Tue, Thu & Fri, to 8pm Wed, 10am–4pm Sat & Sun) refers to a whole district where the legendary Finnish ceramics company has manufactured its products since 1873. The complex, 5km north of Helsinki, includes a design mall, with a large Arabia/Iittala outlet. Take tram 6 or 8 to the Arabiankatu stop.

Best
History

From humble beginnings, Helsinki has gone on to become one of Europe's most visionary cities. These days the capital is so much the centre of everything that goes on in Finland that its obscure market-town past is totally forgotten.

Helsinki was founded in 1550 by King Gustav Vasa to rival the Hansa trading town of Tallinn. Earlier trials at Ekenäs were fruitless, so traders from there and a few other towns were shanghaied to newly founded Helsingfors (the Swedish name). For over 200 years it remained a backwater, though it was razed in 1713 to prevent the Russians occupying it. The inhabitants fled or were captured, and only returned after the Peace of Nystad in 1721.

Later the Swedes built the Sveaborg fortress (Suomenlinna) to protect this eastern part of their empire against further Russian attack. Following the war of 1808, however, the Russians succeeded in taking the fortress. A year later Russia annexed Finland as an autonomous grand duchy. A capital nearer Russia than Sweden was required, so Helsinki was chosen in 1812: Turku lost its longstanding status as Finland's capital and premier town.

In the 19th and early 20th centuries, Helsinki grew rapidly and German architect CL Engel was called on to dignify the city centre. The city suffered heavy Russian bombing during WWII, but postwar Helsinki recovered and hosted the 1952 Summer Olympics. .

Best Historic Sights

Suomenlinna Helsinki's beautiful island-set 18th-century fortress. (p51)

Senaatintori Helsinki's majestic central square with the Tuomiokirkko as its focal point. (p45)

Hietaniemi Cemetery The final resting place of many famous Finns. (p90)

Best History Museums

Seurasaaren Ulkomuseo An outdoor architecture museum set on an island in the archipelago. (p101)

Kansallismuseo The national history museum traces Finnish history from prehistoric times. (p78)

Vesikko submarine, Suomenlinna (p50)

Helsingin Kaupungin-museo Don't miss the excellent city history museum. (p45)

Ratikkamuseo Vintage trams and other bits of historical city life. (p90)

Työväenasuntomuseo A charming little museum depicting the life of early industrial workers. (p108)

Best Historic Houses

Mannerheim-Museo The former home of Finland's one-time president and greatest military hero. (p64)

Amos Andersonin Taidemuseo The publishing magnate's impressive art collection is housed in his elegant Empire-style home. (p88)

Ruiskumestarin talo This Burgher's House shows the life of a 19th-century middle-class family. (p46)

Best Historic Monuments

Memorial to Elias Lönnrot Compiler of the *Kalevala*, the national epic. (p86)

Johan Ludvig Runeberg Statue Memorial to the national poet. (pictured left; p33)

Helsinki Day

Celebrating the city's anniversary, **Helsinki Päivä** (Helsinki Day; www.helsinkipaiva.fi; ⊙11 Jun–12 Jun) brings many free events to the city, with food stalls, concerts, theatre and dance performances, art exhibitions, workshops, cinema screenings, sports events and wellness activities.

Best
Art & Architecture

DMITRY NIKOLAEV/SHUTTERSTOCK ©

Helsinki is the epicentre of Finland's flourishing cultural scene. Inspired by the Finnish wilderness, artists and architects evoked a national pride that fomented a movement leading to the nation's independence in 1917. Venues throughout the capital showcase their talents, along with their successors, as well as emerging artists across the creative spectrum.

Art

Contemporary Finnish art and sculpture plays with disaffection with technological society (think warped Nokias) and reinterprets 'Finnishness' (expect parodies of sauna, birches and blonde stereotypes). Although contemporary art enjoys a high profile in Finland, it is the National Romantic era that is considered Finland's 'golden age' of art. The main features of these artworks are virgin forests and pastoral landscapes. See The Golden Age of Art (p32) for more on specific artists.

Architecture

Helsinki grew up in the early 19th century, when German architect CL Engel made his mark with many noteworthy neoclassical landmarks. Later in the century, art nouveau found inspiration in nature; in Finland, architects such as Eliel Saarinen embraced this international style, here known as National Romantic architecture. Most significantly, Finnish designs gained international renown in the Modern era, when Alvar Aalto and his colleagues embraced the aesthetic of Functionalism. Nowadays, Helsinki continues to be on the cutting-edge of contemporary design and architecture.

Above: Havis Amanda sculpture by sculptor Ville Vallgren

Best Art Museums

Ateneum Finland's premier art gallery, with countless golden-age masterpieces on display. (p24)

Kiasma Exhibits here are complex, quirky and sometimes confounding. (p26)

Helsinki Art Museum Vast exhibition space inside the Tennispalatsi, mainly showing 20th- and 21st-century Finnish artists. (p81)

Amos Andersonin Taidemuseo Shows of the modern collection of the wealthy publishing magnate, with a vast new underground exhibit space coming soon. (p88)

Sinebrychoffin Taidemuseo The former brewing family home contains

Interior of Temppeliaukion Kirkko (p89)

an impressive collection of European paintings. (p65)

Best Architecture

Rautatientori The fabulous train station is a premier example of National Romantic architecture. (p31)

Kallion Kirkko An enormous art nouveau church with amazing acoustics. (p105)

Finlandia Talo Aalto designed every last detail of Helsinki's landmark concert hall. (p96)

Temppeliaukion Kirkko A quintessentially modern-Finnish merger of spirituality and nature. (p89)

Kamppi Chapel An exquisite new addition in wood. (p88)

Best Public Art

Havis Amanda Beloved symbol of the city. (p43)

Sibelius Monument Steel pipes and sound waves memorialise the composer. (p90)

Bear on the Anthill A whimsical depiction of Finland's national mascot. (p104)

Reflections An abstract creation of glass and aluminium. (p105)

Art Island

Kuusisaari island has two excellent private galleries in elaborate villas: **Didrichsen Taidemuseo** (www.didrichsenmuseum.fi; Kuusilahdenkuja 1; adult/child €12/free; ⏰11am-6pm Tue-Sun) and **Villa Gyllenberg** (www.gyllenbergs.fi; Kuusisaarenpolku 11; adult/child €10/free; ⏰3-7pm Wed, 11am-3pm Sat, noon-4pm Sun). Collections include Finnish as well as local and international art. Take bus 194 or 195 from Kamppi bus station or a summer ferry from the kauppatori.

Best
Outdoors

Finland is a nature-loving nation. Even in the city, the great outdoors has enormous appeal, from the Baltic beaches to the archipelago islands to the expansive green spaces on the mainland.

Cycling

With a flat inner city and well-marked cycling paths, Helsinki is ideal for cycling. Pick up the free *Ulkoilukartta* Helsinki cycling map at the tourist office, or view it online at www.ulkoilukartta.fi. Launched in 2016, Helsinki's shared-bike scheme, City Bikes (www.hsl.fi/citybikes), has some 1500 bikes at 150 stations citywide.

Swimming

The Baltic water is brisk, to say the least, but it's pure and refreshing and most Finns are not shy about jumping right in. Take a dip at a popular city beach or opt for a public pool (in which case you can warm up in the sauna afterwards).

Winter Activities

There is plenty of winter to go around, and the Finns know how to get out and enjoy it. Ice skating and skiing are favourite winter pastimes, as is good old-fashioned tobogganing. The Finnish sauna is also critical to surviving Finnish winter.

Best Parks & Gardens

Kajsaniemi Four harbourside hectares of lush gardens. (p28)

Kaivopuisto Rambling waterside park. (p64)

Esplanadin Puisto Helsinki's central strip of green. (p31)

Tervasaari City views, summer theatre and rose gardens bedeck this island park. (p46)

Karhupuisto A small park filled with flowers and whimsical artwork. (p108)

Best Swimming

Allas Sea Pool Open-air swimming pools overlooking the city. (pictured above; p41)

Hietaranta The capital's best city beach. (p89)

Seurasaaren Ulkomuseo Swimming from the rocks or at a naturist beach. (p101)

Best Winter Activities

Jääpuisto Picturesque outdoor ice skating on Rautatientori (Railway Sq; p33)

Kaivopuisto Tobogganing down the slopes is a popular pastime for kids. (p64)

Best Saunas

No matter where you are in Finland, you'll never be far from a sauna (pronounced sah-oo-nah, not saw-nuh). With over two million in homes, hotels, summer cottages, campsites and numerous other unlikely places, saunas are prescribed to cure almost every ailment, used to seal business deals, or just to socialise in over a few beers.

PHOTO: MASTER2000/SHUTTERSTOCK ©

Sauna Etiquette

The sauna is taken naked. While a Finnish family will often take the sauna together, in mixed gatherings it is usual for the men and women to go separately. Public saunas are generally separated by gender.

Sauna Types

The most common sauna is the electric sauna stove, which produces a fairly dry, harsh heat compared with the much-loved chimney sauna, driven by a log fire. Even rarer is the true *savusauna* (smoke sauna), without a chimney. Although the top of a sauna can reach more than 120°C, many Finns consider the most satisfying

temperature for a sauna to be around 80°C.

Sauna Rituals

Use a *kauha* (ladle) to throw water on the *kiuas* (sauna stove), which then gives off the *löyly* (sauna steam). When you are sufficiently warmed, you'll jump in the sea, a lake, river or pool, then return to the sauna to warm up and repeat the cycle several times. If you're indoors, a cold shower will do. The swim and hot-cold aspect is such an integral part of the sauna experience that in the dead of winter Finns cut a hole in the ice and jump right in.

Best Saunas

Löyly Sauna A brand new wind- and water-powered sauna by the sea. (p65)

Allas Sea Pool Swimming pools and saunas in a spectacular setting. (p41)

Kotiharjun Sauna Helsinki's only original traditional public wood-fired sauna. (p108)

Yrjönkadun uimahalli Swimming and sauna amid art deco elegance. (p86)

Sky Wheel Combine sauna and sightseeing on the SkySauna gondola. (p46)

Best
For Kids

Helsinki has a lot to offer kids, with summer boat trips, amusement parks and outdoor events year-round. Finland is a child-friendly society and just about every hotel and restaurant will be keen to help out with cots or high chairs. Family rooms are available even in business hotels.

Best Boat Trips

Suomenlinna Activities at the island fortress include a toy museum and a submarine. (p51)

Helsinki Zoo Encounter a host of animals at the city zoo, spread across the island of Korkeasaari. (p43)

Royal Line Kids under 12 cruise for free on these sightseeing trips. (p138)

Best Museums

Kiasma Loads of opportunity for kids to interact with contemporary art and make their own. (p26)

Luonnontieteellinen Museo Dinosaurs at the Natural History Museum are always a hit with youngsters. (p89)

Kansallismuseo Finland's national museum brings history to life, especially at its hands-on Workshop Vintti. (p78)

Best Aquatic Fun

Sea Life Kallio's aquarium has walk-through tunnels for shark spotting. (p107)

Allas Sea Pool One of the superbly sited outdoor pools is dedicated for kids. (p41)

Hietaranta Golden sands for building castles and safe beach swimming. (p89)

Kaivopuisto A beautiful park with a great beach and playground. (p64)

Best Amusements

Linnanmäki This amusement park has thrilling rides. (p107)

Sky Wheel Kids can identify Helsinki landmarks on this sightseeing Ferris wheel. (p46)

IGOR GROCHEV/SHUTTERSTOCK ©

☑ Top Tips

▶ Local tourist information booklets and websites highlight attractions with family appeal.

▶ Entrance fees and transport tickets for children tend to be around 60% of the adult charge.

▶ Most museums in Helsinki are free for kids.

▶ Public breast feeding is normal practice.

Hohtogolf Minigolf at this indoor complex is played on glow-in-the-dark courses. (p83)

Best
For Free

There are a smattering of free museums around town, while others offer free admission on certain days or at certain times. Among the city's many architectural monuments, the churches are all free to enter and admire. And there's rarely a charge to explore the city's many parks, gardens and beaches.

GRISHA BRUEV/SHUTTERSTOCK ©

Tram Tours

If you're on a budget, you can get a good overview of the city aboard a regular local tram on three main routes, accompanied by free downloadable guides from the tourist office website that briefly describe notable sights along the way. Tram 2 does a classic overview loop, departing from the kauppatori; Tram 4 is a one-way architectural route; and Tram 6 follows a one-way route through the Design District.

Best for Free

Helsingin Kaupungin-museo All branches of the excellent Helsinki City Museum (p45) are free, including Ratikka-museo (p90), Ruiskume-starin talo (p46) and Työväenasuntomuseo. (p108)

Helsinki Art Museum Always offers at least one free exhibition. (p81)

Design Museum There's no charge for the summer pavilion – shared with the Museum of Finnish Architecture. (p56)

Sinebrychoffin Taide-museo Browse this fine-art collection for free in the evening on the first Wednesday of the month. (p65)

Luonnontieteellinen Museo Admission to the natural history museum is free in the afternoon on the first Friday of the month. (pictured; p89)

Kajsaniemi You'll pay to enter the greenhouses but the gardens are free. (p28)

☑ **Top Tips**

▶ Sightsee on foot – many of the city's key sights are concentrated in a compact area and the predominantly flat terrain makes walking easy in amenable weather.

▶ To reduce costs, make lunch the main meal of your day. Numerous cafes and restaurants offer an all-you-can-eat lunch buffet that's far cheaper than dining à la carte.

▶ If you'll be visiting a lot of museums, purchase a Helsinki Card, which includes free city transport and entry into many major attractions.

Best
Tours

If you're short on time, standard hop-on, hop-off bus tours are a handy way to see the sights; tickets are sold at the tourist office. Plenty of companies offer 1½-hour sightseeing cruises, as well as dinner cruises, bus-and-boat combinations and sunset cruises. Pick one up at the quay at the kauppatori.

GRISHA BRUEV/SHUTTERSTOCK ©

Best Boat Tours & Cruises

Helsinki Sightseeing In addition to its 90-minute islands-and-waterways cruise, this company also runs evening jazz cruises, dinner cruises, and bus-and-boat combinations. (Gray Line; ☎09-2288-1600; www.stromma.fl; Kauppatori; ⏱late Apr-late Oct; 1½-hr cruise adult/child €25/13)

IHA Lines Runs cruises along two archipelago routes as well as lunch and dinner cruises. (☎09-6874-5050; www.ihalines.fl; Kauppatori; ⏱late Apr-late Oct; adult/child from €20/10)

Royal Line Great for families, Royal Line offers free cruises for kids aged 12 and under, as well as bus-and-boat combinations. (☎020-711-8333;

www.royalline.fl; Kauppatori; ⏱late Apr-late Oct; 1½-hr cruise adult/child €23/free)

Best Walking & Cycling Tours

Architectural Tours In summer months, the Museum of Finnish Architecture runs excellent architectural tours around the capital. (p62)

Happy Guide Helsinki Runs a range of light-hearted but informative cycling and walking tours around the city. Bike tours include berry picking and sauna tours; walking tours include food tours and craft-beer tours. (☎044-502-0066; www.happyguidehelsinki.com; walking/bike tours from €20/55)

Helsinki Cityride Year-round this outfit offers a variety of walking (or

Nordic walking) tours around various parts of the capital. It also does a three-hour grand cycling tour that passes most of the major sights; prices include bike rental. (☎044-955-8720; www.helsinkicityride.com; tours €45-95)

Best Kayaking Tour

Natura Viva On the island of Vuosaari, east of the city centre, Natura Viva runs daily three-hour paddling excursions around the Helsinki archipelago. It's beginner friendly and pick-ups can be arranged from the centre of town. You can rent kayaks at the paddling centre here. (☎010-292-4030; www.naturaviva.fl; Harbonkatu 13, Vuosaari; ⏱May-Sep; 4½-hr tour €69, kayak hire per 2hr/day €22/40)

Survival Guide

Before You Go   140

When to Go 140

Book Your Stay 140

Arriving in Helsinki   141

Getting Around   142

Bicycle 142

Tram. 143

Metro. 143

Ferry 143

Essential Information   143

Business Hours. 143

Discount Cards 144

Electricity. 144

LGBT Travellers 144

Public Holidays. 144

Safe Travel 144

Taxes & Refunds. 145

Toilets. 145

Tourist Information 145

Travellers with
Disabilities 145

Language   146

Survival Guide

Before You Go

When to Go

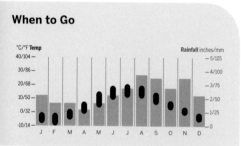

°C/°F Temp
Rainfall inches/mm
40/104 —
30/86 —
20/68 —
10/50 —
0/32 —
-10/14 —

— 5/125
— 4/100
— 3/75
— 2/50
— 1/25
— 0

J F M A M J J A S O N D

➡ **Spring & Autumn**
Best seasons for catching the city in full swing.

➡ **Summer** (mid-June to mid-August) Peak tourist season, but there are closures over midsummer and sometimes in July.

➡ **Winter** Dark and (often) seriously cold, but atmospheric.

Book Your Stay

➡ Helsinki is dominated by chain hotels, particularly Sokos and Scandic, but there are some boutique and designer gems, too. Budget accommodation is in short supply.

➡ From mid-May to mid-August bookings are strongly advisable, although July is a quieter time for business and high-end hotels.

➡ Apartment rentals range from one-room studios to multi-room properties that are ideal for families. Often you'll get use of a sauna, parking area and other facilities.

Useful Websites

City Apartments (www.cityapartments.fi) Offers a variety of central apartments.

Lonely Planet (www.lonelyplanet.com/finland/helsinki/

hotels) Recommendations and bookings.

SATO Hotelhome (www. satohotellikoti.fi) Serviced apartments in several locations for stays of one week or longer.

Visit Helsinki (www. visithelsinki.fi) The tourist board's official website has information and searchable listings.

Best Budget

Hostel Suomenlinna (www.hostelhelsinki.fi) Situated at Finland's island-set fortress, Suomenlinna.

Hostel Diana Park (www. dianapark.fi) Lively location and a laid-back vibe.

Eurohostel (www.eurohostel.eu) Conveniently situated for the Viking Line ferry and an easy walk to the city centre.

Rastila Camping (www. hel.fi) Handy campground with tent pitches and self-catering cottages.

Best Midrange

Hotel Katajanokka (www. hotelkatajanokka.fi) Stunning converted former prison.

Hotelli Krapi (www.krapi.fi) Rustic estate of wooden

buildings with superb amenities and Finnish cookery classes.

Hotelli Helka (www. hotelhelka.com) Streamlined rooms and a super location.

Best Top End

Klaus K (www.klaushotel. com) Striking design and sumptuous organic breakfasts.

Hotel Kämp (www. hotelkamp.com) Venerable antique-furnished beauty.

Hotel F6 (www.hotelf6.fi) One of Helsinki's newest properties, with impeccable environmental credentials.

Hotel Haven (www. hotelhaven.fi) Magnificent harbour views extend from many rooms.

Arriving in Helsinki

Helsinki-Vantaa Airport

Helsinki-Vantaa Airport (www.helsinki-vantaa.fi), 19km north of the city, is Finland's main air terminus. Direct flights serve

many major European cities and several intercontinental destinations.

Finnair (☎09-818-0800; www.finnair.fi) covers 18 Finnish cities, usually at least once per day.

Kamppi Bus Station

Kamppi bus station (www. matkahuolto.fi; Salomonkatu) has a terminal for local buses to Espoo in one wing, while longer-distance buses also depart from here to destinations throughout Finland. From Kamppi bus station, **Onnibus** (www. onnibus.com) runs budget routes to several Finnish cities, including Jyväskylä, Oulu, Savonlinna, Tampere and Turku.

Buses also run from Kamppi bus station to St Petersburg (€35, nine hours, up to four daily); you must have a Russian visa.

Helsinki Train Station

Helsinki's central **train station** (Rautatieasema; www.vr.fi; Kaivokatu 1) is linked to the metro (Rautatientori stop) and situated 500m east of Kamppi bus station. The train is the fastest and cheapest way to get from Helsinki to major centres, including Joensuu, Kuopio, Lappeenranta, Oulu, Rovaniemi, Tampere and Turku.

There are also daily trains (buy tickets from the international counter) to the Russian cities of Vyborg, St Petersburg and Moscow; you'll need a Russian visa.

Ferry Terminals

International ferries sail to Stockholm, Tallinn, St Petersburg and German destinations. Book well in advance during high season (late June to mid-August) and on weekends.

Katajanokan Terminaali

Katajanokan Terminaali, on the island of Katajanokka, is served by trams 4 and 5.

Viking Line (📞 0600-41577; www.vikingline.com) runs car and passenger ferries to Stockholm (16½ hours, one daily) via Åland (11 hours), and to Tallinn (2½ hours, two to three daily).

Makasiiniterminaali

Makasiiniterminaali (Eteläranta 7) is served by tram 1A or 2.

Linda Line (📞 0600-066-8970; www.lindaline.fi; ⏱ Apr-Oct) runs the fastest service between Helsinki and Tallinn, aboard small passenger-only hydrofoils (1½ hours, three daily).

St Peter Line (📞 09-6187-2000; www.stpeterline.com) runs to St Petersburg (14 hours, three weekly).

Olympia Terminaali

Olympia Terminaali (Olympiaranta 1) is served by trams 1A, 2 or 3.

Tallink/Silja Line (📞 0600-15700; www.tallinksilja.com) runs car and passenger services to/from Stockholm (16 hours, one daily) via Åland (11 hours).

Länsiterminaali (West Terminal)

Länsiterminaali (West Terminal; Tyynenmerenkatu 8) is 3km southwest of the city centre, and is served by trams 6T or 9.

Tallink/Silja Line (📞 0600-15700; www.tallink-silja.com) runs car and passenger services to/from Tallinn (two hours, eight daily).

Eckerö Line (📞 0600-4300; www.eckeroline.fi) runs car and passenger

ferries to/from Tallinn (two to 2½ hours, up to three daily).

Hansaterminaali

Hansaterminaali (Provianttikatu 5, Vuosaari) is 18km east of Helsinki, served by bus 90A from Vuosaari metro station.

Finnlines (📞 010-343-4810 www.finnlines.com) runs car and passenger ferries between Helsinki and Travemünde, Germany (29 hours, six to seven per week).

Getting Around

Bicycle

➡ With a flat inner city and well-marked cycling paths, Helsinki is ideal for cycling.

➡ Pick up the free *Ulkoilu-kartta* Helsinki cycling map at the tourist office, or view it online at www.ulkoilukartta.fi.

➡ Launched in 2016, Helsinki's shared-bike scheme, **City Bikes** (www.hsl.fi/citybikes), has some 1500 bikes at 150 stations citywide.

Bikes per 30 minutes/ two hours/four hours are free/€3.50/€7.50. Register online, or pick up a bike at five locations – Hakaniemi metro station, Rautatientori bus station, Kiasma, Kaivopuisto or Unioninkatu – with just a credit card.

Tram

If you're on a budget, you can get a good overview of the city aboard a regular local tram on three main routes: Tram 2, Tram 4 and Tram 6.

From the tourist office website, download free guides that briefly describe notable sights along the way.

Purchase tram tickets onboard, or at sales points such as **Kamppi bus station** (www.matkahuolto.fi; Salomonkatu), many R-kiosks and the tourist office.

Metro

Helsinki has a single, forked metro line and a fast train linking the city to the airport.

From Helsinki train station, trains serve destinations in greater Helsinki and beyond.

Ferry

From the kauppatori (market square), local ferries serve Suomenlinna and Helsinki Zoo, among other island destinations.

Essential Information

Business Hours

Some restaurants, shops and bars close for the summer holidays, although the majority remain open.

Alko (state alcohol store) 9am to 8pm Monday to Friday, to 6pm Saturday

Banks 9am to 4.15pm Monday to Friday

Businesses & shops 9am to 6pm Monday to Friday, to 3pm Saturday

Nightclubs 10pm to 4am Wednesday to Saturday

Pubs 11am to 1am (often later on Friday and Saturday)

Restaurants 11am to 10pm, with lunch 11am to 3pm. Last orders generally an hour before closing.

Dos & Don'ts

Like the rest of the country, Helsinki is a very easy-going place, and visitors are unlikely to be at risk of making any social faux pas.

Greetings Greet men, women and children with a brief but firm handshake and make eye contact.

Small talk Finns value conversation, but don't engage in small talk; silence is considered preferable.

Saunas Shower before entering a sauna. Nudity is the norm (a towel is required in mixed saunas), but check first. Saunas are strictly nonsexual.

Punctuality Finns are very punctual and expect the same in return.

Discount Cards

Helsinki Card (www.helsinkicard.com; 1/2/3-day pass €46/56/66) Gives free public transport around the city and local ferries to Suomenlinna, entry to 28 attractions in and around Helsinki and a 24-hour hop-on, hop-off bus tour.

Helsinki & Region Card (1/2/3-day pass €50/62/72) Offers the same benefits and adds in free transport to/from the airport as well as greater Helsinki destinations, including the satellite city of Espoo.

Electricity

Type C
220V/50Hz

Type F
230V/50Hz

LGBT Travellers

Finland's cities are open, tolerant places. Helsinki has a small but welcoming gay scene and the country's largest pride festival.

Same-sex marriage became legal in Finland on 1 March 2017.

The tourist board website, www.visitfinland.com, is a good starting point for information.

Public Holidays

Helsinki, like the rest of Finland, grinds to a halt twice a year: around Christmas and New Year, and during the midsummer weekend.

National public holidays:

New Year's Day 1 January

Epiphany 6 January

Good Friday March/April

Easter Sunday & Monday March/April

May Day 1 May

Ascension Day May

Whitsunday Late May or early June

Midsummer's Eve & Day Weekend in June closest to 24 June

All Saints Day First Saturday in November

Independence Day 6 December

Christmas Eve 24 December

Christmas Day 25 December

Boxing Day 26 December

Safe Travel

Helsinki is a safe city and travellers exercising common sense shouldn't experience any problems.

➡ The lowest temperature recorded in the city was -34.3°C (in 1987). If you're visiting in winter, it's vital to make sure you have warm clothing and

aterproof boots with
ood grip.

▸ Parts of gentrifying Kal-
o can be sketchy; stick
o busy, well-lit areas
fter dark.

Taxes & Refunds

Value-added tax (VAT) is
evied at 10% for books,
medicines, passenger
ransport, accommoda-
ion services and cul-
ural and entertainment
vents, 14% for restau-
ants and 24% for most
ther items. It should
lready be included in
tated prices.

Non-EU residents may
e able to claim a refund
n a minimum €40 spent
er shop per day. The
ebsite www.vero.fi has
etails.

Toilets

▸ Public toilets are
idespread but can be
xpensive – often €1 a
me.

▸ On doors, 'M' is for men,
hile 'N' is for women.

Tourist Information

Between June and Au-
gust, multilingual 'Helsinki
Helpers' – easily spotted
by their lime-green jack-
ets – are a mine of tourist
information.

**Helsinki City Tourist
Office** (☎09-3101-3300;
www.visithelsinki.fi; Pohjoisesplanadi 19; ⏰9am-6pm
Mon-Sat, to 4pm Sun
mid-May–mid-Sep, 9am-6pm
Mon-Fri, 10am-4pm Sat & Sun
mid-Sep–mid-May) Busy
multilingual office with a
great quantity of information on the city. Also has
an office at the airport.

Strömma (www.stromma.fi;
Pohjoisesplanadi 19; ⏰9am-
6pm Mon-Sat, to 4pm Sun
mid-May–mid-Sep, 9am-6pm
Mon-Fri, 10am-4pm Sat & Sun
mid-Sep–mid-May) In the
city tourist office; sells
various tours and local
cruises, as well as pack-
age tours to Stockholm,
Tallinn and St Petersburg.
Also sells the Helsinki
Card and Helsinki & Re-
gion Card.

Travellers with Disabilities

Helsinki is well equipped
for visitors with dis-
abilities. By law, most
institutions must provide
ramps, lifts and accessi-
ble toilets; all new hotels
and restaurants must
install disabled facilities.
Trains and city buses are
also accessible by wheel-
chair. Ongoing projects
are in place to maximise
disabled access in all
aspects of urban life.

Before leaving home,
get in touch with your
national support organi-
sation – preferably the
'travel officer' if there is
one. The website www.
finlandforall.fi has a
searchable database of
accessible attractions,
accommodation and
restaurants.

Download Lonely
Planet's free Accessible
Travel guide from http://
lptravel.to/Accessible
Travel.

Language

Finnish is a distinct national icon that sets Finland apart from its Scandinavian neighbours. It belongs to the exclusive Finno-Ugric language family, which also counts Estonian and Hungarian as members. There are around six million Finnish speakers in Finland, Sweden, Norway and Russian Karelia. In Finnish, Finland is known as Suomi and the language itself as suomi.

Note that a is pronounced as in 'act', ai as in 'aisle', eu as the 'u' in 'nurse', ew as the 'ee' in 'see' with rounded lips, oh as the 'o' in 'note', ow as in 'how', uh as the 'u' in 'run', and the r sound is rolled. The stressed syllables are indicated with italics in our pronunciation guides.

To enhance your trip with a phrasebook, visit **lonelyplanet.com**. Lonely Planet iPhone phrasebooks are available through the Apple App store.

Basics

Hello.
Hei.   hayn

Goodbye.
Näkemiin.   na·ke·meen

Please.
Ole hyvä.   o·le hew·va

Thank you (very much).
Kiitos (paljon).   kee·tos (puhl·yon)

You're welcome.
Ole hyvä.   o·le hew·v

Excuse me.
Anteeksi.   uhn·tayk·si

Sorry.
Anteeksi.   uhn·tayk·si

How are you?
Mitä kuuluu?   mi·ta koo·loo

Fine. And you?
Hyvää. Entä itsellesi?
                        hew·va en·ta it·sel·le·s

Yes./No.
Kyllä./Ei.   kewl·la/ay

I don't understand.
En ymmärrä.   en ewm·mar·ra

Do you speak English?
Puhutko englantia?
                        pu·hut·ko en·gluhn·ti·u

Eating & Drinking

I'd like ...   *Saisinko ...*   sai·sin·ko ..

a coffee   *kahvia*   kuh·vi·uh

a table   *pöydän*   peu·ew·dan

the menu   *ruokalistan*   ru·o·kuh·lis·tuhr

beer   *pullon*   pul·lon

Cheers!
Kippis!   kip·pis

Do you have vegetarian food?
Onko   on·ko teyl·la
teilläkasvisruokia? kuhs·vis·ru·o·ki·uh

I'll have a ...
Tilaan ...   ti·laan ...

I'd like (the) bill please.
Saisinko laskun.   sai·sin·ko luhs·kun

Shopping

I'm looking for ...
Etsin ...   et·sin ...

How much is this?
Mitä se maksaa?   mi·ta se muhk·saa

It's too expensive.
Se on liian kallis   se on lee·uhn kuhl·lis

It's faulty.
Se on viallinen.   se on vi·uhl·li·nen

Emergencies

Help!
Apua!   uh·pu·uh

Call the police!
Soittakaa   soyt·tuh·kaa
paikalle poliisi!   paikalle poliisi

Call a doctor!
Soittakaa   soyt·tuh·kaa
paikalle lääkäri!   paikalle la·ka·ri

I'm lost.
Olen eksynyt.   o·len ek·sew·newt

Where are the toilets?
Missä on vessa?   mis·sa on ves·suh

Time & Numbers

What time is it?
Paljonko kello on?   puhl·yon·ko kel·lo on

It's in the ... Kello on ...   kel·lo on ...

morning   aamulla   aa·mul·luh
afternoon   iltapäivällä   il·tuh·pa·i·val·la
evening   illalla   il·luhl·luh

Monday   maanantai   maa·nuhn·tai
Tuesday   tiistai   tees·tai
Wednesday keskiviikko   kes·ki·veek·ko
Thursday   torstai   tors·tai

Friday   perjantai   per·yuhn·tai
Saturday   lauantai   low·uhn·tai
Sunday   sunnuntai   sun·nun·tai

1	yksi	ewk·si
2	kaksi	kuhk·si
3	kolme	kol·me
4	neljä	nel·ya
5	viisi	vee·si
6	kuusi	koo·si
7	seitsemän	sayt·se·man
8	kahdeksan	kuhk·dek·suhn
9	yhdeksän	ewh·dek·san
10	kymmenen	kewm·me·nen
100	sata	suh·tuh
1000	tuhat	tu·huht

Transport & Directions

Where's the...?
Missä on ...?   mis·sa on ...

bank   pankki   puhnk·ki
market   kauppatori   kowp·pa·to·ri
post office postitoimisto
pos·ti·toy·mis·to

Can you show me (on the map)?
Voitko näyttää   voyt·ko na·ewt·ta
sen minulle   sen mi·nul·le
(kartalta)?   (kar·tuhl·tuh)

How much is it to ...?
Miten paljon   mi·ten puhl·yon
maksaa matka ...?   muhk·saa muht·kuh ...

Behind the Scenes

Send Us Your Feedback

We love to hear from travellers – your comments help make our books better. We read every word, and we guarantee that your feedback goes straight to the authors. Visit **lonelyplanet.com/contact** to submit your updates and suggestions.

Note: We may edit, reproduce and incorporate your comments in Lonely Planet products such as guidebooks, websites and digital products, so let us know if you don't want your comments reproduced or your name acknowledged. For a copy of our privacy policy visit lonelyplanet.com/privacy.

Mara's Thanks

Kiitos a million times over to my Finnish family, Outi and Kauko Ojala, for their in-depth knowledge of Finland, for their never-ending hospitality and for so many laughs over the course of 30 years. Here's to 30 more! *Kiitos* another million times to my American family – to my parents, who keep coming back for more; to my kiddos, for their ever-adventurous spirits; and to my favourite travel companion of all time, for accompanying me on this fabulous journey.

Catherine's Thanks

Kiitos paljon/tack så mycket first to Julian, and to all of the locals, tourism professionals and fellow travellers who provided insights, inspiration and good times. Huge thanks too to destination editor Gemma Graham, my Finland and Scandinavia co-authors, and all at Lonely Planet. As ever, *merci encore* to my parents, brother, *belle-sœur* and *neveu*.

Acknowledgments

Cover photograph: Skating in front of the Ateneum, Peter Adams/AWL©

This Book

This 1st edition of Lonely Planet's *Pocket Helsinki* guide was curated by Mara Vorhees and researched and written by Catherine Le Nevez. This guidebook was produced by the following:

Destination Editor: Gemma Graham

Product Editors: Bruce Evans, Anne Mason, Genna Patterson

Senior Cartographer: Valentina Kremenchutskaya

Book Designer: Jessica Rose

Assisting Editors: Andrew Bain, Charlotte Orr, Gabrielle Stefanos, Amanda Williamson

Cover Researcher: Naomi Parker

Thanks to Virginia Moreno, Kirsten Rawlings

Index

See also separate subindexes for:

⊗ **Eating** p151

🍷 **Drinking** p151

☆ **Entertainment** p152

🛍 **Shopping** p152

A

alto, Alvar 63
ccessible travel 145
ccommodation 140-1
ctivities 134
inola 114-15
rports 141
coholic drinks 124
llas Sea Pool 41
mos Andersonin Taidemuseo 88
rabiakeskus 129
rchitecture 63, 118-19, 132-3, **119**
rt 132-3
rt galleries 132-3
rtists 32
teneum 24-5
TMs 16

B

ars 124-5, *see also* Drinking *subindex*
athrooms 145
eaches 89
ear on the Anthill 104
eer 125
icycle travel 142-3
oat travel, *see* ferry travel

Sights 000
Map Pages **000**

botanical gardens 28-9
budgeting 16
bus travel 141
business hours 143

C

cell phones 16
ceramics 128
children's attractions 136
Churberg, Fanny 32
City Centre 22-37, **30**
    drinking 34-5
    entertainment 35-6
    food 33-4
    itineraries 23
    shopping 36-7
    sights 24-5, 26-7, 28-9, 31, 33
    transport 23
classical music 126-7
climate 140
cocktail bars 125
coffee 124, 125
costs 16, 144
cruises 41, 46, 138
cuisine 122
currency 16
cycling 134, 138

D

dangers, *see* safety
design 72

Design District 58-9, 72, 75, **58**
Design Museum 56-7
Didrichsen Taidemuseo 133
disabilities, travellers with 145
discount cards 144
drinking 124-5, *see also* Drinking *subindex*, *individual neighbourhoods*
drinks 124

E

Edelfelt, Albert 32
Ehrensvärd-Museo 51
electricity 144
emergencies 147
entertainment 126-7, *see also* Entertainment *subindex*, *individual neighbourhoods*
Esplanadin Puisto 31-3
etiquette 143
events, *see* festivals & events

F

fashion 128
ferry travel 142, 143
festivals & events 111, 131
food 122-3, *see also* Eating *subindex*,

individual neighbourhoods
free attractions 137

G

Gallen-Kallela, Akseli 32
gardens 28-9, 120-1, 134, **121**
gay travellers 144
glassware 128

H

Halonen, Pekka 32
Halosenniemi 115
HAM Metro 81
Hartwall Arena 127
Havis Amanda 43
Helsingin Kaupungin-museo 45
Helsinki Art Museum 81
Helsinki Distillery Company 108
Helsinki Päivä 131
Helsinki Zoo 43-5
Hietaniemi Cemetery 90
Hietaranta 89
highlights 8-11, 12-13
historic houses 131
historic sites 130
history 44, 130-1
holidays 144

I

icebreaker fleet 41
ice-skating 33
itineraries 14-15, *see
also individual
neighbourhoods*

J

Jääpuisto 33
Järnefelt, Eero 32
jazz 127
Johanneksenkirkko 62

K

Kaivopuisto 64-5
Kajsaniemi 28-9
Kalevala 87
Kallio 102-11, **106**
  drinking 110-11
  entertainment 111
  food 108-10
  itineraries 103, 104-5
  shopping 111
  sights 107-8
  transport 103
  walking tours 104-5,
    104
Kallio Block Party 111
Kallion Kirkko 105
Kamppi & Töölö 76-99,
  84-5
  drinking 94-6
  entertainment 96-9
  food 90-4
  itineraries 77, 82-3
  shopping 99
  sights 78-9, 80-1,
    86-90
  transport 77
  walking tours 82-3,

82
Kamppi Chapel 88-9
Kansallismuseo 78-9
Karhupuisto 108
Katajanokka, *see*
  Kruununhaka &
  Katajanokka
kauppatori 48, 118
kayaking 138
Kiasma 26-7
Kotiharjun Sauna 108
Kruununhaka &
  Katajanokka 38-49,
  40, **42**
  drinking 48
  food 46-8
  itineraries 39, 40-1
  shopping 49
  sights 43-6
  transport 39
  walking tours 40-1,
    40

L

language 16, 146-7
Lelumuseo 53
lesbian travellers 144
Linnanmäki 107
literature 87
local life 12-13, *see also
  itineraries, walking
  tours*
Lönnrot, Elias 87
Lottamuseo 115
Löyly Sauna 65
**Luonnontieteellinen
  Museo 89**

M

**Majakkalaiva
  Relandersgrund 41**
**Mannerheim-
  Museo 64**
Mäntynen, Jussi 104
Merikasarmi 41

metro travel 143
minigolf 83
mobile phones 16
money 16, 144
monuments 131
**Museum of Finnish
  Architecture 62**
museums 130-1, 132-3
music 126-7

N

National Romantic
  era 32
nightlife 124-5

O

**Observatory Hill
  Park 62-4**
Olympic Stadium 90
opening hours 143

P

parks 120-1, 134, **121**
**Parliament
  House 89**
planning 16
politics 44
Porvoo 112-13, **112**
Porvoo Museum 113
Presidentinlinna 43
Punavuori & Ullanlinna
  54-75, **60-1**
  drinking 71-4
  entertainment 75
  food 65-71
  itineraries 55, 58-9
  shopping 75
  sights 56-7, 62-5
  transport 55
  walking tours 58-9,
    58

R

Rantakasarmi 50

Ratikkamuseo 90
Rautatientori 31
red storehouses 113
Reflections 105
Rissanen, Juho 32
rock music 127
**Ruiskumestarin
  talo 46**

S

safety 110, 144-5
Sallinen, Tyko 32
Sanomatalo 31
saunas 65, 108, 135
Schjerfbeck, Helene 32
Sea Life 107-8
Senaatintori 45
**Seurasaaren
  Ulkomuseo 100-1**
shopping 128-9
Sibelius, Jean 37
**Sibelius Monument
  90**
Simberg, Hugo 32
**Sinebrychoffin
  Taidemuseo 65**
Sky Wheel 46
**Sotamuseo Maneesi
  53**
sports 126, 127
street parties 111
Suomenlinna 50-3, 52
**Suomenlinna-Museo
  52**
**Suomenlinnan Kirkko
  51**
swimming 134
Symbol, The 105

T

taxes 145
taxis 17
telephone
  services 16

Sights p000
Map Pages **p000**

emppeliaukion
   Kirkko 89-90
ennispalatsi 80-1
ervasaari 40
heatre 126
ckets 94
me 16
pping 16
bilets 145
öölö, see Kamppi &
   Töölö
op sights 8-11
ourist information 145
burs 137, 138, see also
   walking tours
ain travel 141-2
am travel 143
ansport 17, 141-3
avel to/from
   Helsinki 17, 141-2
avel within
   Helsinki 17, 142-3
uomiokirkko 45, 113
uusulanjärvi 114-15
yöväenasunto-
museo 108

llanlinna, see Puna-
vuori & Ullanlinna
spenskin
   Katedraali 45

anha Kirkko 86
egetarian travellers
   123, 146
esikko 52
isas 16
on Wright brothers 32

alking tours
   architectural 118-19,
   119

Design District
   58-9, **58**
Kallio 104-5, **104**
Kamppi & Töölö
   82-3, **82**
Kruununhaka & Kata-
   janokka 40-1, **40**
parks & gardens
   120-1, **121**
Punavuora & Ullan-
   linna 58-9, **58**
weather 140
websites 16, 140-1
Wickström, Emil 32
winter activities 134
World Peace 105

Y
Yrjönkadun
   Uimahalli 86

⊗**Eating**

A
Anton & Anton 47-8
Ask 47
Ateljé Finne 92

B
Bellevue 48
Brooklyn Cafe 70
Brunberg sweet shop 113
B-Smokery 110

C
Café Bar 9 71
Cafe Postres 113
Cafe Regatta 90
Café Ursula 68
Carelia 92

D

Demo 66

E
Emo 33-4

F
Fafa's 70-1
Flying Dutch 109

G
Gaijin 68-9
Goodwin 70
Grön 83
Grotesk 68

H
Hakaniemen Kauppa-
   halli 110
Helmi Tea & Coffee
   House 113
Hietalahden Kauppa-
   halli 92

J
Juuri 68

K
Kanniston Leipomo 34
Karl Fazer Café 33
KarlJohan 92-3
Kitch 92
Kolme Kruunua 47
Konepahalli 70
Konstan Möljä 93
Kosmos 91
Kuja 108
Kuu 91

L
Lappi Ravintola 93

M
Mumin Kaffe 47

N
Naughty Brgr 93-4

O
Olo 46

R
Ragu 69
Rupla 105

S
Saaga 67
Saaristo 123
Salve 93
Saslik 67-8
Savotta 48
Savoy 66
Savu 46-7
Sea Horse 70
Silvoplee 110
Skiffer 69-70
Soppakeittiö 66
Story 66
Strindberg 33
Suomenlinnan
   Panimo 125

T
Teurastamo 105
The Cock 68
Tin Tin Tango 93

V-W-Z
Vanha Kauppahalli 65-6
Wanha Laamanni 113
Zucchini 69

🍷 Drinking

A21 94
Andante 74
Ateljee Bar 95
Bäkkäri 95-6
Bier-Bier 73
Birri 72
Corona Baari 83
DTM 96
Fairytale 111
Good Life Coffee 110
Hercules 96
Holiday 48
Johan & Nyström 41
Kaffa Roastery 71
Kaivohuone 72
Kappeli 34
Konepahalli 70
Kuudes Linja 110-11
La Torrefazione 34
Liberty or Death 73
Los Cojones 74
Mattolaituri 73
Maxine 95
Porvoon Paahtimo 113
Raffaellon Terassi 34
Roskapankki 111
Steam Hellsinki 94
Teatteri 34-5
Teerenpeli 82
TheRiff 73
Tommyknocker
  Helsinki 73
U Kaleva 96
Vin-Vin 94

🎭 Entertainment

Bar Loose 83
Finlandia Talo 96
Helsingin Jäähalli 97-8
Hohtogolf 83
Juttutupa 111
Kansallisteatteri 36
Musiikkitalo 35
Nosturi 75
Oopperatalo 98
Orion Theatre 96
Semifinal 83, 97
Storyville 98-9
Tavastia 83
Telia 5G Arena 97

🛍 Shopping

Aarikka 37
Akateeminen
  Kirjakauppa 37
Alnilam 99
Artek 36
Art.fi 59
Awake 59
Bisarri 58
Domus Classica 75
Fargo 105
Fennica Records 111
Frank/ie 75
Iittala 36-7
Jukka Rintal 59
Kalevala Koru 37
Kuuma 58-9
Lasikammari 49
Levykauppa Äx 99
Lokal 59
Mafka & Alakoski 59
Moomin Shop 99
Nide 59
Roobertin Herkku 75
Scandinavian Outdoor
  99
Schröder 41
Stockmann 37
Sweet Story 49
Tre 36

Our W

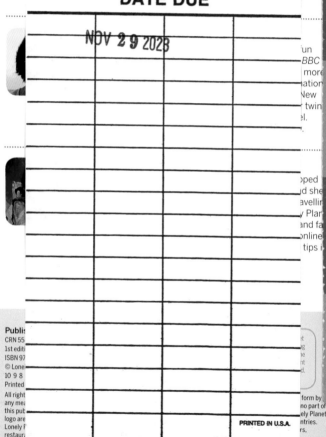

un
BBC
more
ation
New
twin
el.

oped
d she
avellin
y Plar
and fa
online
tips i

Publis
CRN 55
1st editi
ISBN 97
© Lone
10 9 8
Printed